THE
Quintessential
GUIDE
ON
HOW TO *DO MORE*
OF
WHAT YOU LOVE
FOR *ENTREPRENEURS*

RAQUEL GREENE

ELOHAI
INTERNATIONAL
PUBLISHING & MEDIA

Published by ELOHAI International Publishing & Media

P.O. Box 64402
Virginia Beach, VA 23467

ElohaiIntl.com

For bulk requests, contact Hello@ElohaiIntl.com

Library of Congress Control Number: 201895599

ISBN: 978-1-7324971-4-6

Printed in the United States of America

DEDICATION

dedicated
to
the most sincere
cheerleaders,
full of
wisdom
honesty
laughter
love
and joy unspeakable

Ollieopo

TABLE OF CONTENTS

INTRODUCTION

I KNOW. You already think you're organized. You already have systems in place.

When I used to work for Bell Atlantic, everyone had red binders on their desks. Affectionately known as "The Red Book," this binder was our go-to guide for nearly everything. When we didn't know an answer to a customer question, "The Red Book" is where we would go. Once I left that job, I started creating red books for the CEOs that I supported. These red books became office bibles of sorts, because when I was away, these high-level executives didn't know what the daily operational procedures were.

In my head, a starting point for organization and increased productivity is creating a red book for everyone, and the beginning of that process is to identify the purpose and contents of that book. It will be different for every entrepreneur and CEO.

The Quintessential Guide is going to provide you with the beginning steps to help you organize your business—not just in terms of filing papers, but also establishing order to every aspect of your life as an entrepreneur. I'm going to teach you the quintessential steps to become more efficient, eliminate time-wasting habits, and create more time to do the work you love. Once you're done, you will have the tools to create your own red book.

I know that many entrepreneurs *dread* the administrative stuff, and they'd rather pay someone to do this. If that's you, I get it, and I'm here for you. Reach out to me at greener@qexecs.com. Although administration work may not be exciting work per-se, this is the stuff that will help make your days and your business more successful, not just day-by-day, but for the long-haul. My advice is to go through this guide, do what you can, and let me know how I can help you with the rest.

If you're the spouse, assistant, or loved one of an entrepreneur, this book will be the PERFECT gift to help them start and finish strong. So, let's get to it!

Chapter 1:

CREATING A LIFE YOU LOVE

How to Create a Life You Love

Loving your life allows you to bring your best to every interaction. It's not selfish to want to have a life you love. Most of my steps to creating a life I love have benefited the people *in* my life as well. The truth is that most of the time, life is ordinary. Yes, there are times of pain. However, by consciously taking these steps, you will create a life you love and become a person that other people love to be around.

If you are an entrepreneur, there is something that you have a passion to do. You've decided that you want to create, build, and share your passion with the world. This doesn't mean that your business will be the only responsibility that you can successfully handle in the beginning. Many entrepreneurs do not have the freedom to do what they love full-time (in the beginning), while also earning a living. So what happens is that the dream becomes the "side hustle," and we ambitious entrepreneurs continue working full-time jobs. The question that many entrepreneurs face is, "How do I create a life I love?" And the follow-up, "How can I do this full time?" This chapter will explore both.

Has there ever been a time in your life when you didn't know that you could actually make your own choices or *how* to make them? Most people live off of a list that our parents, our families, and sometimes our friends have created and unfortunately in the end we choose what *they* expected of us.

A *respectable career* to most parents (when I was growing up and even still today) means medicine or law, a teacher or any type of "secure" nine-to-five position. The problem is that nowadays, these positions are not-so-secure... (but that's an entirely different book).

Sadly, we often realize that who we have morphed into does not reflect our own truest, most authentic self. We live lives that others have planned, and we are miserable, uninspired, unfulfilled, and we crave something more, something more... *us*! Kinda' like living life and wearing someone else's clothes. Too big, too small, nothing just right.

When most of us daydream about the "perfect" life, we want a life full of all the people and things we love, and we want to spend our time doing what makes us happy. We see ourselves taking our passions, all the things we're good at, and making our passions our careers. We tend to make choices that reflect our values and hearts. The problem is that we only live uninhibited in our dreams—inside of our own heads. We don't trust ourselves to live that way out loud. We don't trust ourselves.

We become so programmed to do and be people we are not. At some point, you (all of us) must take a step back and look deep inside of yourself. Are you afraid to take the necessary steps to live the life you want?

You may have to walk away from everything you have become to be who you really are designed to be. You must be strong, and it is going to require courage.

It's time to wake up and be honest...with yourself...

It definitely isn't easy, and it isn't a quick fix. In fact, working on yourself is a lifetime commitment. The good news is that the knowledge and skills you have gained through your process will be critical to your health and growth. You're going to need everything you have to become everything you were created to be.

SAY GOODBYE TO DOING IT ALONE.

I can tell you that you can't go through this entrepreneurial journey alone. You will need someone to hold you accountable for your dreams, insecurities, fears, and your actions. You may need someone who will make you promise to yourself that you will do what is in your heart to do.

Combining our passions with our careers should come easy. We have a right to do what we love, but for many of us, it's more difficult than we could have ever imagined. We literally don't realize that we have the right to choose. For others, "success" has arrived (along with the big checks, big cars, and big houses). Even though this group of people may feel unfulfilled and unhappy, the thought of walking away and starting over is unfathomable. Public "success" hides private misery.

What would happen if you were taught to make choices that affect your LIFE with your spirit instead of your head?

What would happen if you started to visualize your dreams and could see them in front of you? You'd be surprised.

ASSIGNMENT FOR YOU...

1. Get out a piece of paper and start writing. This is an exercise in honesty and integrity.

2. Write: How do you feel about your career, your relationships, your family, your body, your fitness, your health, your diet, or any other areas of your life?

3. If any of these areas of your life are not a number ten on a scale of one to ten (ten being the best it could be) why not?

4. What are you going to do right now to change them?

5. Are you living your purpose and if no, why not?

6. How do you know when you aren't living the life you love? Are you stuck in something that has no passion?

7. Are you just burnt out and in need of inspiration?

If you spend more of your time *unhappy* than you do feeling fulfilled and inspired, you probably need to reevaluate your life. If you are afraid to leave your career and create something of your own because you fear what others will think of you—or because you are concerned with disappointing someone in your life—then it's time to consider who has the control over your choices.

My greatest realization was that this is MY life and I get to write the story! I get to decide how much time off I need to nurture myself and give back in a meaningful way. I get to decide how to rejuvenate and replenish my soul.

CREATING THE LIFE YOU LOVE DOES NOT HAVE TO BE OVERWHELMING.

To create a life you enjoy living, you must be willing to let go of outdated passions and get rid of patterns and people that are no longer serving your biggest desires and dreams. Surround yourself with inspiring and uplifting people who won't allow you to settle for anything less than living a life connected to all that you love.

Are you ready?

MENTAL HABITS YOU NEED TO QUIT TO LIVE A LIFE YOU LOVE

Has your heart ever ached for something more? Sometimes you are on the right path, yet, your mental habits stop you from seeing the truth. People are often blinded to the fact that life is a journey and so is finding and living in passion and on purpose.
What habits are blinding you?

Check the list below to see if any of these issues have caused you to become misaligned with your vision.

1. Excuses

Most stories begin with excuses. Deep down, we know what we should do next.

But often, our own thoughts, such as the ones below hold us back:

- I'm not good enough.

- I don't know enough.

- I haven't found the perfect passion.

- Who would want to listen to me?

- I don't have the connections.

- I don't know where to start.

- What if this ends up being a waste of time?

Eventually, you have to face the fact that if you want to move forward, you must do it despite the excuses roaming around in your head. You must break free from your self-imposed prison.

There is never anything holding you back. You are always in charge of the thoughts in your head, and YOU GET TO CHOOSE which thoughts will have power. Let go of your excuse-making habits starting today.

You will have to move from focusing on what *could* go wrong to asking yourself "what tiny step can I take next?" Better yet, consider what could go right.

Focus on what you can do with what you have and realize that all you ever need to do is to follow what inspires you... and, take the next step. It's that simple! It is not easy, nor is the path always clear.

2. Perfectionism

This is the act of wanting to get everything just right, so no one can criticize or judge you. Perfectionism translates to you protecting yourself against the world.

Deeper than that, you are making the dangerous assumption that you *have to* protect yourself from something. Perfection is a great (imaginary) ideal, but not an achievable goal. You are always growing and improving. You will never be perfect, and that's part of the beauty of life.

You can only ever do your best. Following your heart is your job. Controlling life, and other people, is not. One realization that will help you deal with perfectionism is remembering that entrepreneurship isn't about instant perfection, but about constant progress.

3. What Will People Think?

Hand-in-hand with perfectionism is the habit of worrying about what people will think of you.

When I started out, I avoided broadcasting on live video via Periscope or Facebook because I was afraid that my friends would see what I was up to and think it was silly.

Today, I see how silly fear made me for valuing others' opinions over my own dreams.

The truth is that people don't care about what I do, and I mean that in a good way. They have their own lives to live. However, even if people have negative opinions about what I'm doing, it does not and should not change how I live my life. I'm not going to let someone else stop me from following my passion and living the life for which I am destined. People can say what they want, but I'll keep doing what I love.

4. I'm a Fraud.

As my business has grown, so has the responsibility I have to my customers and clients.

I worry about not knowing enough, not helping people enough.

This mental habit is beneficial as long as it doesn't prevent me from moving forward. It shows that I care about what I do and the people I help.

Here's how I deal with feeling like a fraud. I like to get out my notebook and ballpoint pen. I investigate the feeling. I ask myself questions such as:

- Specifically, is there an area where I need to know more or do better?
- What am I doing well?
- What have I learned in the past year?
- What can I do to become better right now?
- Is this vague feeling of not being good enough helpful?

You may not be as good as you want to be at *everything*, but you're great at what you *do* know. That makes you good enough. You will never stop learning, which means you can never know everything. You can only ever share what you know, and that's enough.

"We have to dare to be ourselves, however frightening or strange that self may prove to be."
- Mary Sarton

5. Comparing Yourself to Others

There are people out there who will know more than you.
That's fine.

However, comparing yourself to others is a lie, because no one is like you. You are not here to walk the path of someone else. Your purpose does not look like anyone else's out there. You will have to walk into the forest and create your own path.

You have to be willing to trust your heart and see where it takes you. Work with what you have. Deal with your insecurity of not being enough. You may feel both fear and joy, because they are two sides of the same coin.

6. Yearning for Results

Next up is the dangerous assumption that the more you achieve, the happier you will be.

I used to work around the clock, thinking that I'd achieve my goals faster. But all I did was squander my time. As I've relaxed, I've noticed that the less I force, the happier I am, and the faster I make progress.

Be here now. I do my best to find enjoyment in the present moment. I work for work's sake. If I'm doing something I don't want to do, I bring my mind back to the present moment, and things become easier. Focus on what's important.

7. Avoiding Struggle

"If someone is determined not to risk pain, then such a person must do without many things: having children, getting married, the ecstasy of sex, the hope of ambition, friendship – all that makes life alive, meaningful and significant. Move out or grow in any dimension and pain as well as joy will be your reward. A full life will be full of pain. But the only alternative is not to live fully or not to live at all."
- M. Scott Peck

Life is difficult. However, the problem isn't the difficulty of life, but resisting it.

The more you resist life, the more you suffer. The more willing you are to face struggle, the more it melts away. What matters is not what life delivers, but how you react.

In my life, I've noticed that what I've initially believed to be negative events actually lead me to my passion, to my calling.

"How shall my heart be unsealed unless it be broken?"
- Khalil Gibran

You must rise above difficulty and struggle. Enjoy both the sweet and the bitter of life.

You will not always succeed, but do your best, and each day, you will become better.

8. Living Logically

I'm talking about the mental habit of wanting to live life logically. You can plan. Make lists. Try to figure out the future, but life doesn't care about your plans. I don't know where my life is going.

You cannot plan for a future you've created in your own mind. You can only listen to the song of your heart, and follow the positive pulls of your soul.

For example, when I thought about writing this book, I felt open, relaxed, and happy. It's not a side gripping kind of happy, but a subtle opening up of my heart.

> *"Although the road is never ending*
> *take a step and keep walking,*
> *do not look fearfully into the distance…*
> *On this path let the heart be your guide*
> *for the body is hesitant and full of fear."*
> **- Rumi**

My body may be full of fear, but my heart knows where to go. It doesn't give me a map. It gives me the next step, and I move forward.

So here's the thing.
You can be afraid… and confused, and at the same time, follow your passion, and do work you love.

But you must be willing to start before you *feel* like you're ready, before you have a perfect plan. With each step, you will grow to trust yourself and trust life. You don't know what's coming? That's okay! You don't have to know.

All you have to do is take the next step.

Creating a life you love begins with these important steps:

1. Take responsibility for your own actions.

Take responsibility for your own actions and results. Yes, there are jerks out there and stuff happens. However, if you can try to own and understand your own part in every single thing that happens to you, you actually gain power.

In my life, I've had a couple of not-so-pleasant relationships. I could easily blame others for being jerks. Yet, with self-awareness and analyzing the part I played (and the red flags I blatantly ignored!), I learned and accepted that I played a part in my own bad experiences.

Usually, in any experience of mine that doesn't go well, I can pinpoint some of my own actions that contributed to my own results. Of course, it's easier to see these in hindsight. I like to think that by taking responsibility for my own actions, I'll be better prepared the next time to make better decisions. Better decisions in the now create better results in the future!

2. Forgive and forgive often.

Along with accepting my own part in any situation or relationship, forgiving is probably the most essential thing I do. In fact, forgiving is such a cornerstone to the way I live.

The biggest lesson I had to learn was that forgiving is not to benefit the other person or to say that what they did is okay. It is for our own personal benefits. Forgiveness will allow you to release the emotions and avoid the same situations in the future.

When you hold onto crap that people did to you, you keep it active in your *own* body, mind, and soul. Have you ever wondered why the same things keep happening to you over and over? It's because you haven't resolved the issues yet. You haven't passed the tests.

Taking responsibility for your part and forgiving the other parties go a long way in clearing that stuff out.
My mother often reminds me, "Unforgiveness is like drinking poison and waiting for the other person to die."

3. Actively look for ways to be thankful.

I am so thankful that my parents taught me to actively look for ways to be thankful. They were openly appreciative of anything beautiful, different kinds of people, their families, the blessings they received. They did not live a charmed life. They experienced challenges and setbacks as most families do, but they always looked for the beauty in every situation.

4. Talk through the negative things instead of complaining about them.

Sometimes life happens, and we can't sugar coat a bad experience or ignore it. However, you can decide not to let terrible events disable you more than they have to. Excessive complaining keeps you in that negative place.

Stay positive about life and continually look for gems to appreciate and for which you can be thankful.

My parents taught me to see beauty, love, and value in ordinary things: a beautiful garden, the love of a special pet, and with the people in our lives.

My mom especially can find something to appreciate in the most mundane of things: a cup of coffee, a Payday candy bar, a bite of something delicious, or a call from one of her grandchildren.

5. Release and get out of toxic relationships. Here's how:

Embrace forgiveness, appreciation, and love. While you're building a business and creating a life you love, you need positive people around you. Part of being an entrepreneur is being in a creative space. The opposite of that is when you have toxic people and things in your creative space.

Everyone loves a happily ever after. As girls, we grew up reading fairy tales and dreaming of Prince Charming. From a romantic perspective, even when relationships go awry, we always believe that everything's going to turn out okay in the end. We desperately want to believe that the happy couple will stay in love and live "happily ever after," as they ride off into the sunset.

But in the real world, people are not nearly as idealistic, idealized, or just plain ideal as they are in the pages of your favorite novel or on the big screen of those sweet romance comedies. Our relationships in business are also not that simple. People have bad habits, attitudes, and problems that prevent relationships from becoming everything they could be. In reality, when we take off the rose-colored glasses, relationships and people in romance and in business can become toxic.

So why do we stay or tolerate such behavior knowing that it will impact our livelihood and creative headspace?

The answer: walking away is hard. Why? Because, being alone is a scary proposition for most people. Even the biggest introverts long for human interaction, affection, and affirmation at times. But when a relationship turns toxic, the best move you can do for you is get out. I've compiled a list of seven reasons why you need to let go of toxic relationships. If you'd like to download a copy and be empowered in your journey toward healthier relationships, visit qexecs.com/letgo.

6. Follow your own compass.

This is your life to live. Sometimes we buy into how we need to live because so many other people are doing it. We buy houses, drive cars, choose jobs, and have certain relationships based on what is culturally accepted.

While none of these things may seem inherently good or bad, many of us are on autopilot about what we should do and when. It takes true courage to live even a little bit outside of the box. However, it is outside of the box where the creativity begins. It is only by following our own compasses in our own time that we create that special feeling of being comfortable in our own skin which is essential to creating a life you love.

7. Nurture your relationships.

Some people are better at this than others. You may like people and be fairly social but forget birthdays and important dates or get paralyzed over what to do when someone is going through bad times.

Make the conscious decision to do better. Call people. Make plans to get together. Really *really* try to remember important dates. Relationships usually don't end because of one thing. They often end because of long periods of neglect. My relationships are truly one of the reasons I live a life I love. I nurture relationships with family, with friends, and with co-workers. All relationships don't have to be of the best friend quality, but all can be healthy and enriching.

8. Express yourself.

Learn how to express yourself daily. Find new ways to express deeper parts of yourself. Journal. Paint. Whatever allows you to release whatever is inside. Writing has taught me to express myself in personal relationships better.

It's tough sometimes to say what we mean or to say what we want. I believe in being polite. I also believe it's important to express the truth as best we can. Speaking your truth leads to conversations and opportunities you couldn't have otherwise.

9. Take care of your body.

Your body is the vehicle that you'll need to get you to a life you love. It's fairly resilient for a while, but without proper care it begins to break down and get sick. We are seeing that happen at earlier ages these days.

When I was growing up, almost every kid was healthy, thin, active, and energetic. I don't remember any kids who were obese. We didn't have special diets, and most of us weren't involved in organized sports.

That was then.
So here it is (and you already know this, but...), eat healthy. Exercise. Drink water. Your body will thank you.

10. Reach beyond "I can't" and "I don't want to" and have fun!

Over the years, I have avoided doing or learning certain things. I can't even tell you how many things I haven't done because of the belief that I couldn't or that I didn't want to.

However, FUN dwells in doing things that are beyond the road blocks of "can't" and "I don't want to." Do things that make you happy. Make you smile. Make you laugh with joy.

At each opportunity, go beyond what you thought you couldn't do or what you thought you didn't want to do. You will expand your life experiences and create a joy that is indescribable!

Q-Tip #1: Don't participate in these behaviors if you want to do more of what you LOVE.

- Don't procrastinate.

- Don't settle.

- Don't share all of your dreams with other people.

- Don't be afraid.

- Don't self-sabotage.

- Don't doubt yourself.

- Don't speak negative over your vision.

- Don't be afraid to invest in the life you love.

Chapter 2:
ORGANIZATION

"I am a mind-reading, color coding, banner-waving, cape-wearing hero that would love to use my super powers to drive your cause forward." Is this you... in your daydreams or in reality?

Everyone is not organized, although they think they are. In this chapter, let's find out if you are *really* organized or if you have a misperception of "organization."

Some people say, "I live better with clutter" or "This is my organized chaos and I know where everything is!" While you may have learned to operate in that chaos, it's not the best way to maximize your creative space, both mentally and physically.

How often does life seem chaotic to you?

If you're like me—working a full-time job, starting your business, managing family obligations— life can feel pretty chaotic sometimes.

Some people are energized by the chaos. Others are totally thrown off by the chaos. As an entrepreneur, it's important to make sense of the chaos in order to truly succeed.

Though some chaos will inevitably creep into any day, there are certain tricks and "hacks" that can keep you organized *no matter what.*

An entrepreneur's goals are its guiding lights. Every successful entrepreneur *has* goals, and the *most* successful entrepreneur reviews his or her goals frequently, if not daily.

Keeping your goals front and center allows you to weave through the chaos. It's a process that helps you chip away at the extra details. It can reveal what is important, what is a waste of time and what you should do about it all.

To instantly bring organization and clarity to life, some like to batch tasks. "Batching" is collecting all of your similar tasks for the day (or week) and doing them all at once.

Email: Do them all at once (within reason re: time).

Writing articles: Get it done in a single afternoon.

Writing your business plan: Take a morning and write it down.

Many have learned that after batching, they become ten times more productive. Batching can eliminate your disorganization in one fell swoop. Work on the one thing that will move your business forward.

For most entrepreneurs, there's that *one thing* in your mind that you know you should do. You recognize its importance and even realize that it has the potential to change your business and dramatically move things forward.

The problem? You feel too disorganized to do it.

A simple way to usher organization into your life is to just *do it*. Every day when you wake up, resolve to do at least *one task* that will move your business forward.

Doing so will organize your thinking and your priorities. It will give you a clear and coherent vision for the success of your business.

Two Business Hacks of SUPER Organized Entrepreneurs:

1. Choose a few major tasks for the day.

Staying organized is as much about what you choose *not* to do as it is about what you choose *to* do. Choosing too many "priorities" for the day will crush you and leave you gasping for relief. Before you know it, your day will crumble into a pile of disorganized chaos.

The secret to staying on track?

Select a few tasks that you *need* to get done for the day. Maybe it's a single task—an article, a marketing plan, one step towards a new hire, etc.—that you *must* get done.

They are the major tasks you want to get done this week.

Unfortunately, these tasks often get pushed back from week-to-week because we never have time to do them—our days fill up too quickly.

How do you avoid this problem? By planning your week with the critical tasks first.

2. Delegate.

For the becoming (or evolving or growing) entrepreneur, it's delegate or die. In fact, the art of delegation may be the difference between entrepreneurs who flounder and entrepreneurs who succeed.

Delegating gets harder to do the higher someone moves up the corporate ladder. Delegating can be even more difficult for the entrepreneur.

A few tips to move from anti-delegator to master delegator.

1. Understand why you're not delegating.
2. Measure how you're doing.
3. Choose the right people.
4. Integrate delegation into what you already do.
5. Ask others to hold you accountable.
6. Really let go.
7. Learn from experience.

Here are some of the responsibilities that entrepreneurs must learn to delegate:

Anything you don't enjoy doing.

Anything you don't do well.

Anything that will help to increase cash flow.

Anything that is getting in the way of growing your business.

Anything that is process-oriented (easy to do) but time consuming.

Anything you want a team member or aspiring leader to learn to do.

If you run all your tasks through this delegation matrix, you may discover you're left with very little to do.

What does this mean? Have you delegated too much? No! Instead, you've unlocked the secret to mastering entrepreneurship. You've freed yourself of administrative minutiae and can take your business to extraordinary new heights.

Entrepreneurs *must* be organized. Does this mean that they always iron their shirts in a certain way and live life by a routine schedule? Maybe not, and that's okay.

The point is an entrepreneur organizes his or her life around what's important—growing the business and achieving their dreams. If you attempt this task without a thought as to organization, you'll fail. If you guide your tasks with an organized mindset, you will succeed. And since I can read your mind, I know some people are thinking "I may be unorganized, but my business is still growing and making money." That may be true. My response to that mindset is *but what are you losing as a result?* Also, how much more success could you have with a few processes in place?

Disorganization - does it really matter?

Many studies have shown that disorganization can indicate intelligence and creativity, explaining why some people excuse their clutter as a "creative mess." Although a chaotic environment might work on a personal level for certain types of people, it can destroy a business if left unchecked.

Lack of organization goes well beyond measurable losses, negatively affecting a company's reputation, a chance for growth, or competitive edge, all the while increasing stress levels and lowering workplace morale. Here you will begin to learn to what extent disorder can be detrimental to your business as a whole.

In the business world, time is the most valuable commodity. While trying to save time, you might forget to identify and eliminate time-wasting activities. A study conducted by Harvard Business School illustrates this point through data; out of 18,000 business leaders, fifty-seven percent said they lose six working hours per week as a result of disorganization. Disorganized employees who earn $50,000 annually cost their companies an additional $11,000 in lost time.

Disorganization can take many forms. Simple activities such as searching for misplaced tools, supplies or computer files quickly add up to become serious time wasters that cause distraction and dramatically affect productivity. Even though the time spent searching for items is generally not perceived as a waste, when translated into actual costs and multiplied, the tangible losses prove to be significant.

Let's talk about some…

Missed Opportunities

The costs associated with missed opportunities due to poor organization happen daily. Missed deadlines can cause cost overruns or lost business deals. When remembered, details about product specifications, terms of sale, or terms of employment make your business successful. When overlooked or forgotten, details become an expensive liability.

Scattered attention causes many to misunderstand their objectives and waste resources. Failure to prioritize tasks often results in employees falling short of goals and failing to fulfill their purposes. Disorganization can also cause communication failures that lead to expensive redundancy or lack of clarity in team efforts, which in turn generates even more missed opportunities.

Businesses need well-defined goals and established priorities to create environments that foster innovation and growth. Similarly, companies need to inspire confidence in the hearts and minds of their existing and potential clients or business partners to maintain a reputation of excellence and professionalism. Disorganization jeopardizes everything.

Stop missing opportunities by making sure everyone on your team (including vendors and the like) understands the purpose of your company, as well as the roles and responsibilities they have to ensure its long-term and short-term success.

Higher Stress Levels

Whether physical or procedural, lack of organization leads to situations that increase stress levels. A chaotic working environment leaves people constantly wondering who they report to and what they are supposed to do while at work, leading to workload discrepancies and disengagement. This applies even if you work alone. Even entrepreneurs rely on help from time-to-time. If you're not clear on objectives and timelines, they won't be either.

Attack stress at its roots by removing clutter from your environment. Establish a filing system for your physical and digital documents so that you and your colleagues can find material without the need for frustrating searches. By creating a practical organizational structure and implementing clearly identifiable and understood policies and procedures, you will be able to focus your energy on what truly matters.

Money Down the Drain

The cost of disorganization in your business will inevitably lead to measurable losses in profitability. Consider how much replacing lost tools, recreating lost files, or paying late fees cost your business. Think of the losses involved with forgetting to send invoices to customers, paying for overtime labor, and dealing with employee turnover. Stop throwing money away. Take steps to organize your business and stop its financial bleeding.

Disorganization wastes money. You might think you lack the necessary time to reduce clutter and impose order in your business. When you realize the amount of money your company loses while searching for items, missing opportunities, and feeling stressed, you might want to reconsider your time allocation. The time spent getting organized will deliver a handsome return on that investment.

Six Tips to Get Organized

If done properly these tips will improve anyone's productivity. These six steps have made me a better entrepreneur. The results are different, but they are not varied. Organization improves the quality of our lives, the quality of our work, the quality of our teams, and the quality of our selves. If this is what you want (and I can't imagine a reason why anyone would not want to try to achieve those goals), implement these principles into your life:

1. When you're in a conversation, be *in* the conversation.

Be here now. How many times do other people ask you to look them in the eye or to pay attention to them when you're speaking to them? Are you distracted? Are you looking at something on your phone? Are you daydreaming about your next big book idea? It seems to be common practice in today's society that our attention is constantly taken away from what is right in front of us. If you are going to talk to others, then give them the courtesy of having your *full* attention. It will prevent the possibility of miscommunication and reduce the probability of having repeat conversations, another time waster.

2. Find a method of accountability that works for you and use it.

If you truly want to be organized, then you need to hold your feet to the fire. You can't be lazy about acting in this endeavor. It will not work, and you will rarely get around to accomplishing your priorities.

Organization is action. Finding a method of accountability is as simple, or complicated, as finding a system of delivery that works for you.

3. Stay connected without disconnecting from those around you.

It is very important to stay connected in every meaning of the word. We all live very busy lives. We have many different responsibilities that pull at us. We struggle with finding the right mix of how to spend our time. We too often either end up neglecting our duties in our businesses or neglect our connections to the people we love.

4. Get rid of all distractions from the task at hand.

One of the most difficult achievements to accomplish, even though we all try, is staying on task. In the world we live, there are so many different distractions that can take us away from what we need to get *done* and with whom we want to *connect*.

5. Make use of every minute you have.

Don't waste time. So much work is neglected because business owners do not want to get to it. So much work is put off because it is not due for many days in the future. What ends up happening is stuff either goes undone or it gets done, but not very well.

6. Keep it short and simple (K.I.S.S.).

Do not over-complicate processes. Do not give too many absolutes. Let there be some room for the imagination, and let your statements breathe. And don't perform overkill on simple tasks that must be done every single day. Keeping it simple will help you to remember how it should be done, and it will help you remember the overall structure and process of whatever it is you're organizing.

Organization, to me, is success. If you can achieve it then you will not only be happier, but you will be more productive. This will increase your earning potential as you free up time to do what really matters. Apply these principles and you will find the success that you seek. You just have to be consistent.

THE QUINTESSENTIAL GUIDE FOR ENTREPRENEURS

WHAT *TO DO* immediately?

Here are seven quick low-cost tips to get organized:

1. Create a place for everything.

2. Establish a designated place to work.

3. Create a color-coding system.

4. Throw away the clutter - DO NOT be a hoarder!

5. Purchase the software you need.

6. Make lists for everything. I have created color-coded to-do lists, lists of goals, etc.

7. Use one calendar.

Q-Tip #2: Organized entrepreneurs review their goals DAILY.

Chapter 3:

TIME MANAGEMENT

As an entrepreneur, you know that time equals money. As we address time management in the chapter ahead, I have a quick spoiler alert. The gist of this chapter is that setting boundaries is VITALLY important.

It's not uncommon for entrepreneurs to have another main source of income in the beginning. In fact, according to www.fitsmallbusiness.com, eighty percent of entrepreneurs use their own money to fund their businesses and only 6.02% of business owners use it as the sole source of income. If you are one of those entrepreneurs (or even if you aren't) you will need to master time-management in order to be productive in both places.

Many find themselves trying to squeeze time at their full-time jobs to manage their businesses, then, after traffic, family duties, etc., they are too tired to build their businesses during the times when they are not at work. Don't be the person who is too tired to build your dream. Instead, learn to manage your time by creating boundaries in three key areas: relationships, time, and goals.

"No is a complete sentence."

Why Boundaries?

It's easy to let your company time run over into your personal time. You want to do a good job, but it's important to have a cut-off time and a designated space where you work; determine what that needs to look like. Set boundaries for how you manage your business time and/or when you will leave work each day. You will have to learn how to say no.

Relationship Boundaries

"Boundaries are necessary for a successful relationship. Most relationships are aborted in the "boundary defining" stage. Not because people demanded what they needed. But because they didn't, then got resentful about it."
- Karen Marie Moning

Starting a business is a perfect time and opportunity to begin to set boundaries that will help you build stronger relationships and reach your goals and aspirations. For instance, you may find that you have several groups of friends. Childhood friendships, while cherished, are not always the relationships that will support your journey of building a business. You may need to find networking groups to be a part of instead. It doesn't mean you completely disconnect. You just establish boundaries and define for yourself friend vs. work zones. Invest extra time to building relationships with like-minded people. Unfortunately, sometimes you will have to throw the whole friendship away. It's a hard pill to swallow, but sometimes there are people who were only meant to be in your life for a season. Even more importantly, there are some toxic relationships that you have (friends, family, business) that cannot go with you on this new path you're creating for yourself.

Time Boundaries

If you don't already, the more you share your business, you will begin to receive invitations to all types of events, workshops, conferences, panel discussions, brunches… If you're a new full-time entrepreneur, your family may mistake your time in front of the computer as "free time" where you can run errands or talk to them on the phone. Discipline will go hand-in-hand with creating time boundaries. Set your "work hours" and stick to them. Limit the amount of time you are out socializing unless it will truly impact your business in a positive way. Know your seasons. Sometimes, especially in the earlier seasons of your business, it's best to spend time at the desk rather than networking, and in later seasons, you might find it beneficial to network and meet new people by attending events. Use wisdom and plan accordingly!

Tips to Make it Happen

- Plan the night before.
- Plan for the unexpected.
- Schedule time to strategize every six months or annually.
- Make your yearly goals happen by implementing strategy and planning.
- Figure out how to handle your phone calls and emails so that they don't back up. My advice is to schedule a time for both. Perhaps each day from 10-11 a.m. and 4-5 p.m. you check your email account and voice messages and respond to people who've contacted you.

Setting up your Day

I set up my day the night before. You may not realize how much you really have to do until you write it down. Imagine having to complete ten tasks (that were surprises that popped up) before the main task that you planned to accomplish that day. It's also motivation to wake up "on time" for work if you know there's a full list of tasks.

> *"Nothing is so fatiguing as the eternal hanging on*
> *of an uncompleted task."*
> **- William James**

Common Mistakes Entrepreneurs Make with Time

How well do you manage your time? If you're like many people, your answer may not be completely positive! Perhaps you feel overloaded, and you often have to work late to hit your deadlines. Or maybe your days seem to go from one crisis to another, and this is stressful and disheartening.

Many of us know that we could be managing our time more effectively, but it can be difficult to identify the mistakes that we are making and to figure out how we could improve. When we manage our time well, however, we're exceptionally productive at work, and our stress levels drop. We can devote time to the creative, high-rewarding projects that can make a real difference. Basically, we're happier!

What Mistakes can you avoid?

Failing to keep to-do lists - Sometimes I can't sleep well at night for thinking about all the tasks I didn't do today, should've done last week, and must be done tomorrow. Keeping a list is a way of acknowledging what must be done, even if it's not right now. Having it on paper ensures that I won't forget about it and I can go to sleep in peace.

No personal goals in sight - You should always know where you'd like to be in six months, one year, and five years down the road. It doesn't mean you will have every point detailed. These goals will simply keep you motivated and moving. There will be some challenging days and having an end in view can motivate you.

Not prioritizing - As an entrepreneur you will wear several hats at once. Every now and then you will need to hire a contractor that will also need some of your time. Your deadlines will multiply as your business grows. Everything will seem like an emergency. When you prioritize your day and your task list, you will not only know what to tackle first, you will also be able easily identify tasks that can wait.

Failing to manage distractions - Have you ever heard somebody say they can actually get all of their work done in four-to-six hours? Then what are the other hours used for? Distractions! Time you spend catching up with friends, ordering lunch, making dinner plans, scheduling your next dentist appointment... And the list goes on. Distractions aren't always bad, but they don't help with the tasks at hand. It's okay to handle your personal life, but do it with a time limit. Don't look up at the end of your work day to realize that you haven't crossed off one task from your to-do list. You're wasting time and losing money, simultaneously.

Poor scheduling techniques - As an entrepreneur you must be in touch with yourself. You need to know if you work better before dawn or if you're a night owl. When I lived at home, this was so important for me and my mom. I am a night owl. The later it gets, the more I turn up. My mother, on the other hand, is an early riser. The conflict would come because we both had work to do. I would want to have brunch and chit chat and leisurely saunter into my afternoon. But when I did that I was robbing my mom of her most productive hours. Often, after we had talked and had coffee, made the grocery lists etc., she was done. Unfortunately, she would feel like she hadn't accomplished much for the day. We had to put time limits on certain hours during the day so that we could both feel accomplished at night.

Busy being busy - You've heard of busy work, right? Well, being busy doesn't equal actual work being done or money being made. Some people get a rush on being busy, being seen, being in all the "right" meetings. But behind closed doors, they rarely meet deadlines, always ask for extensions, never answer emails on the first request, and only get work done at the eleventh hour, consistently. They operate on adrenaline and are addicted to "busyness." This person is not effective nor productive.

> *"My advice is to never do tomorrow what you can do today. Procrastination is the thief of time."*
> ### *- Charles Dickens*

Are *YOU* a Procrastinator?

Does this sound familiar? You decided to take a fifteen-minute coffee break and couldn't find your favorite coffee mug. Instead of using what was in front of you, you decided to organize the cabinets, so you could be more efficient. You later realized that an hour passed and you had to rush to complete the tasks on your to-do list. Similarly, what about the time you decided to clean your desk drawers while searching for your favorite pen. Before you know it, you were collecting old supplies and working on an impromptu craft project with your kids?

So, what's wrong with organizing your cabinets, cleaning your office, or having craft time with the kids? Nothing. You are definitely getting stuff done—just not the right stuff.

When you run your own business, procrastination may look like avoiding uncomfortable callbacks or prolonging challenging meetings, or habitually showing up late, or taking long breaks, even before you really accomplish anything. You may also find yourself getting stuck on a task and refusing to move ahead.

Why do entrepreneurs procrastinate?

No Established Priorities

It is very easy to start day-dreaming in the middle of a morning call or meeting. You could be thinking of what your spouse is cooking for dinner that day or about planning your next meeting with a client and everything in between. If you think this isn't a problem, you are wrong. This type of procrastination is the worst kind because everyone suffers from it to some extent. You are ignoring important tasks by going after more manageable, easier, and ultimately less-important tasks.

Failure to Set up Deadlines and Rewards

Getting the job done on time is easy to confuse with doing a good job. The two are very different. Getting the job done will create a level of relief after a prolonged period of stress. But when the job is done well, you experience euphoria. You not only want to meet the deadlines, you want to exceed the quality of the output. And when you've done that, you can allow yourself to enjoy the success of it.

Lack of Motivation

When people first start a business, the energy is so high. They get to create marketing material, make calls, meet new people, and sometimes hire staff. But once that is all in place, the work begins. Initially it may even feel boring. It's because the reality of the work hits. That feeling will definitely fade as the average entrepreneur will realize he or she is now doing what they love to do. There are many days when motivation is needed to push forward.

No Accountability

This is another reason why many people procrastinate. Of course, for the entrepreneur this will be hard to deal with because you are the boss. And for some people that is why we wanted to start our own companies, so we don't have to answer to anybody. But after a period of time, that fails. You can always justify not working, leaving early, putting things off, because there's no one to audibly say "get back to work."

So, is there a cure or is this a part of the entrepreneur's personality that he or she should just accept? The answer, of course, is "yes" there is a cure.

Step #1

Ask yourself these two questions every time you feel the urge to shift your focus to a different task:

A - What's the most important problem that needs to be addressed *now*?
B - Am I working on it? If not, then why not?

Step #2

Once you have prioritized your work, it is time to set up personal deadlines that are stricter than the actual deadlines. I always build in a few days, whenever possible, for my deadlines. If I know Friday is the absolute latest, in my head and my memos, I say Wednesday is the deadline. If something comes up and I have to move the date, I am still in safe distance to complete my task on time. In the event I get done early, it just allows me to start on something else, ahead of schedule. I may even have time to take a break.

Step #3

The most effective cure is probably to simply stay motivated. It's important to keep yourself healthy, both emotionally and physically. Exercising is a great way to do this. But you must be mentally motivated too. Keeping your achievements before you is a great way to do that. Always remember why you do what you do.

Step #4

Be accountable. There must be somebody to whom you answer. For example, you can share your week's goals with your VA. By Wednesday, this person can check in with you to see where you are on your list for the week. Obviously, you're "in charge," but sometimes just the idea that you know someone will ask you about a task is motivation enough.

Q-Tip #3: You will increase your confidence with every new accomplishment. Make accomplishing something your first goal each day.

Chapter 4:

TAKE CARE OF YOU FIRST. ME! ME! ME!

"How you do one thing is how you do everything."
- Suzanne Evans

Self-care, self-management, self-aid, personal care… Regardless of your word choice, it's all the same thing and it deals with how (the way) you take care of yourself. I love how the Oxford Dictionary defines it:

"Self-care /self /ker/ **noun** *(self-care)*
The practice of taking action to "preserve or improve one's own health".

Self-care is for anyone who wants it.

It can be as easy — and as free — as taking a walk, or as complex as learning a trade.

Self-care can include, but is not limited to, saying no; buying things, refusing to buy things, taking a long walk, helping others, exercising, crafting, stockpiling, and organizing items like coins and arranging them meticulously into Ziploc bags, stretching, listening to disco, spending time alone, singing karaoke (sometimes, alone); intending to one day start meditating.

This chapter addresses why we as entrepreneurs must tend to ourselves first. Often, we will sacrifice everything for sake of starting a business. It's almost as if the neglect equates to a personal level of commitment to the new venture. When actually caring for ourselves, staying mentally and physically strong, is just as much a part of the business plan as is the business. Don't wait for someone else to do it for you.

> *"There are days I drop words of comfort on myself*
> *like falling leaves and remember that it is enough*
> *to be taken care of by myself."*
> *- Brian Andreas*

Ever notice how your actions carry out and their actual effects on your life? Sometimes, to get your business off the ground, you have to get your home life straight first. If you're running late for all of your personal meetings, it's definitely running over in your calendar. If you can't stay on task with priorities at home, you will not be able to stay on task in business. I believe that entrepreneurs must put first things first and that means pay attention to the personal priorities.

Often, entrepreneurs find themselves running late for work, the salon, the gym, getting to the bank just in time, etc. If you have other responsibilities while you get this business off the ground, be sure that your business is productive as it should be by eliminating your personal clutter. What does that look like for you? What are your most important items? How can you get your personal life organized so that you can identify the available time for you to work your business?

Eighty percent of entrepreneurs use their own money to fund their business from outside employment (AKA a full-time job). If that's your scenario, you have limited "extra time." You need to make the most of your evenings and weekends. And to do that, you need to have a schedule of sorts for your personal errands and responsibilities that cannot wait. Sometimes that may even mean, giving up an evening or a Saturday morning to tend to these tasks. Initially it may seem like you are giving away valuable time, time that you don't have. But really, getting it done and off your plate will free up your time and headspace. I'm reminded of this every time I fly. The stew-ardess stands in the aisle and proceeds to walk me through what to do in case of an emergency. She demonstrates the correct way to use the oxygen mask. The statement that always rings loud to me is when she says, "If you're traveling with a child or someone who requires assistance, secure your mask on first, and then assist the other person." Why is that? Because it is understood that you can't help anybody if you're not completely functional yourself. What's even more fascinating is that if you tried to work and assist without your face mask on and proceed helping others, you potentially would begin to lose your ability to recognize faces and shapes, and eventually pass out. It's the same in business. When our bodies and minds aren't rested, we may operate and possibly appear to be winning. But eventually our sight (vision) gets blurred. Then, what seemed like a wildly successful business launch will turn into a barely average plateau.

Here are some tips to begin to organize your personal life:

Unclutter your space. (It's hard to be creative in a cluttered space.)
Schedule your personal life on your calendar first. (Taking care of yourself first means that you will schedule your important personal affairs prior to adding on new responsibilities.)
Implement personal care. (What does this look like for you? It's different for everyone! You definitely need to plan time to wind down and take care of you.)

Nourish your mental, financial, and spiritual priorities.

Everyone can use a bit more self-care. The best way to do this is to implement small self-care habits every day. I had a counselor suggest I do something delicious! An activity just for me. It was to be an investment on which only I would receive the return.

Below are two types of self-care, inner and outer self-care. You want to take care of *all* of you. Here are a few things you can do that are low in cost and won't take long.

Inner Self-Care

- Make a date with yourself. Spend an hour alone doing something that nourishes you (reading, your hobby, walking around the neighborhood, visiting a museum or gallery, etc.). This does not include work or checking off your to-do list.

- Read books and watch movies you enjoy.

- Paint or write something that lets out your creative energy.

- Unplug. Turn off everything, including social media.

- Journal.

- Learn something new, research something you're interested in.

- Meditate.

- Take a class for fun. Take up a foreign language if you want!

- Take a quick power nap. Ten-to-twenty minutes can refresh you.

Outter Self-Care

- Eat something you enjoy.

- Have a long bath or shower, sit around in your bathrobe, and read magazines.

- Do one thing just because it makes you happy.

- Declutter (mini version). Recycle three pieces from your wardrobe that you don't love or regularly wear or clean out your purse.

- Help someone else. Carry a bag, open a door, or call a sick friend.

- Stretch. Five-to-ten minutes will relieve tension and help your body and mind.

- Run or walk for a few minutes. Get your heart rate up.

- Give your body comfort. Take a hot bath. Use a special lotion or fragrance that makes you happy.

- Spend time with real friends and other people who lift you up.

"Nourishing yourself in a way that helps you blossom
in the direction you want to go is attainable, and you are worth
the effort."
- Deborah Day

Here are the Top Self-Care Activities that Every Entrepreneur Needs to Incorporate into His or Her Daily Living:

1. Rest! This is so important while you're trying to get a new project off the ground.

2. Make time for fun. Spend time with your family and friends. Make laughter a regular part of your regiment.

3. Take time off, rejuvenate. There are so many free and low-cost ways to do this. Maybe you can't afford a spa day, but why can't you create one at home? Could you go to the beach and meditate as the waves crash in the background. Have you taken time to walk outside and appreciate nature? All of these activities will foster your creativity and allow you to appreciate your down time.

4. Have an end to your workday. There must be a daily "clock out" time. Allow yourself time to disconnect.

5. Stay healthy. It's hard to inspire others or be creative if you lack energy. Exercise!

Q-Tip #4: Write down the top seven activities you enjoy for self-care. Plan to participate in one activity each day of the week.

Chapter 5:

OFFICE

"When I said that I cleaned my office,
I just meant I made a path from the doorway to my desk."

Does that describe you? What does your office space look like? Working from home is an awesome perk, but if you haven't organized and decorated it, you may be working in a place that feels similar to the cubicle you just ran away from.

Many entrepreneurs work from their couches, kitchen tables, or bedrooms. While this is not totally bad, you will be more productive if you have a designated office space and office hours. There are benefits of having office space, whether in your own home or a designated off-site office. A space that you have to actually go into encourages entrepreneurs to be punctual in their businesses. It adds a level of accountability for daily tasks and helps with creativity. A designated office space provides the mental impression that we are getting up and going to work or into the office, with specific office duties, assignments, appointments, and goals to accomplish for the day.

This space will help you be creative, daydream, and get inspired. If you're just starting out, don't stress yourself out. Your "office" space can be a small nook in the corner of your kitchen! When you separate your office time and space, it will help you focus on the tasks at hand.

There are so many positives to working from home — work-life balance, no commute, and the best part (I think) is my own creative cove, customized just for me. No longer do I have to lug around an iPod loaded with mood music, extra charger cords, family pictures and frames, favorite vases, and my favorite coffee mug to make my space "feel" like me, running the risk of damage to my belongings or worse someone playing hide and go seek with my stuff. And let's not forget the carefully prepared lunch bags, with all kinds of notes with my name plastered on every flat surface, hoping no one eats my lunch as their morning snack.

If you're working from home now, it's time to create your safe haven… Here's how to create a home office that you'll actually want to work in.

1. Use Pinterest.

Pinterest has become my go-to resource if I need some inspiration on colors and designs. You can browse, but always remember to create a space that makes sense. When we visit model homes or scan through magazines we must remember that those designs don't always make the best sense for actually working. They're good showrooms, but that's about it. Upholstered dining room chairs are fabulous, but do nothing for your back after several hours of answering emails upright. Tiny vintage desks don't have the space needed for your files, supplies, etc. A good home office needs to be functional first and beautiful second.

2. Be ergonomically correct.

You didn't leave the ball and chain of a nine-to-five to develop carpal tunnel working from home!

According to Hannah Newman from "Greatest" (online blog), "The top of your computer screen should be at eye level or a little below. Position your keyboard so your forearms are parallel to the floor.

And adjust your chair so your feet rest firmly on something–the floor, or a footrest if you're short."

Also, splurge on your office chair. It needs to be good for more than great pics for your website. You want a chair that makes you want to put in the hours. It sounds obvious, but you should love the chair you're sitting on. Otherwise, you will never sit at your desk.

3. Embrace natural light.

When you place your desk in your home office, if you're like most people, you will place it against a wall or in a corner…. all with good intentions. Because your goal is to get the most out of the space you have. However, what you have done is created a homemade cubicle! And who wants that? Try to position your desk near your windows, if you have them in this space. This will give you the benefits of natural light, and you don't have to leave your space to take in the scenery.

4. More storage please!

Filing cabinets aren't the most attractive pieces of furniture, but you need a place to put papers and files. The biggest issue with home offices is that you wind up having paper everywhere. Some people are extremely hands on. Therefore, having neatly organized files tucked away would drive them crazy. So, if you must *see* your work, consider investing in some desk organizers or hanging media files. Another option is what most people would call cubby holes, individual blocks that can be stacked with supplies, files, etc. You can even buy baskets for each cubby hole to contain the clutter, for those "I-can't-throw-this-out-yet" items. If you need book cases, get nice ones–big enough that you don't need to overstuff, and artsy enough that they'll look great as the backdrop in your video conferences.

And lastly, if you're using a space that doubles as your guest bedroom, that's okay too. Since it's a bedroom, you can use the closet as a major storage source. Use shelving units and baskets, and you will minimize the need for storage in the main office (the bedroom) area. It keeps it sleek for guests when you have them and maintains order for your business.

6. Build your nest.

Your desk is for active work, but you probably need a place to think or read, too. A great home office has at least one piece of nice comfy furniture for curling up to read a book, listen to tapes, or just to brainstorm, a creative space away from your structured desk area, when you want to "get away" without leaving your office.

7. Hide what you don't want to look at.

Most offices have lots of cords and chargers everywhere. Use power strips behind your desk and plug everything into that. Use your Wi-Fi and remote options for your office equipment. Printers, fax machines, and scanners can go in the closet. If there is no closet, there are some creative and inexpensive covers that you can buy to camouflage the equipment.

8. Overstock.

If your work hours are during times when everybody is home (in the evening after your nine-to-five, for example) you don't want to have to leave your office for everything. (Often, once they see you, you must be off the clock). Keep all your office supplies–pens, scissors, stapler, stamps–handy. You may want to even consider a small fridge or coffee maker if you like to enjoy a few beverages during the day (these are especially inexpensive during the months before college students return to school). But the fridge shouldn't be used for every-thing. You need a reason to leave your space at some point during the day, to stretch your legs.

Office Hours

We spoke about boundaries in business in chapter three when we discussed time management. Establishing office hours helps you to create distinct boundaries between your professional life and your personal life (family, fun, fitness, faith).

Ideal Environment

Some entrepreneurs work best around others. However, when many of us start businesses, we don't have the luxury of having coworkers and colleagues with which to interact. If you're that person who gets energized by the presence of other people or even working in public, identify a few spaces that you can incorporate into your work schedule. These places include coffee shops, co-working spaces, libraries, or even parks.

There are other creative ways to work. Some fun options to consider include purchasing a standing desk, a tension ball that you can sit on, or an exercise bike that provides room for your books or laptop.

Your office needs to be a space that helps you be more productive and creative, but it can be (and should also be) fun. Create a space that inspires you to do more of what you love!

Let's be honest, some of you reading this information are thinking "all these tips are great…if I had a brand-new space I was working with. But my space is too far gone…"

If you want a few things you can do TODAY, try these favorites:

1. Throw something away! (old newspapers, magazines, etc.)
2. Stop buying excessive office supplies that you never use.
3. Create a place for everything. Start making the piles of paper make sense.
4. Move out items that are unrelated to work.
5. Recycle. For the things you hate to throw out, create a box for a local business school for students that may need supplies (This could be a possible tax write-off for you too!).

Even creative spaces need rules…

Office Rules: These items should NOT be in your office! [HINT: Distractions!]

Earlier in the chapter, we discussed establishing office hours. If you are working your business on the side, there are some activities that you absolutely should not do while you are working your business.

Here are my Quintessential Tips!

1. No logging onto social media to check Instagram, Facebook, The Shade Room, or other social sites.
2. No working on other non-business-related work!
3. No personal phone calls.
4. No television, unless it's essential to your business.
5. No excessive eating or full-fledge meals "on the job."
6. Limit the time you will spend responding to emails. Perhaps you will establish a time limit on checking emails (i.e. thirty minutes every four hours).
7. Establish a business phone line so that you can separate your personal calls from business.

Q-Tip #5: If your home is your castle, your "office" will be your empire! Treat it as such.

Chapter 6:

STRESS MANAGEMENT

There's something about the entrepreneurial personality type that leads to success. An energetic, enthusiastic entrepreneur can just keep going and going. When other people are ready to throw in the towel and quit, this type of personality will redouble existing efforts instead. In the end, it's *this* approach to starting and maintaining a business that can lead to massive success.

At the same time, though, there are two sides to this coin. The entrepreneurial personality is prone to depression, anxiety, and ultimately, major burnout. Without a balanced approach to starting and running a small business, the stress and anxiety can spiral out of control.

This chapter will help you personally manage stress and prevent burnout in your professional life…

Management Tools

Some entrepreneurs think that because they're flying solo, there's no need for management tools. After all, you're wearing all of the hats, right? So why waste time trying to set up a bunch of complicated to-do lists when you could just knock out the work and be done with it?

The truth is that regardless of whether you're managing a list of tasks or a team of people, using software programs and other tools is always a good idea. You can't possibly juggle everything in your head and keep track of it all. Trying to keep up with that level of detail is an unnecessary stressor. Management programs allow you to clearly differentiate between tasks, organize them by due date, and set up steps for their completion. If you're not well-versed in which software would be most beneficial, you can hire a virtual assistant to help you with these tasks.

Automation

Whenever you find yourself doing something that feels unnecessarily tedious, it's worth asking yourself: Is there a better, easier, automated way of accomplishing this?

More often than not, there is. Automation can save your business hundreds of hours of time, which translates to a ton of money saved. It may seem like a lot to do in the beginning. But once the systems have been created and are in place, your to-do list will instantly become shorter.

Work-Life Balance

At the end of the day, time is our most valuable resource. A lot of entrepreneurs are workaholics who "live to work" and fail to devote enough time to rest and relaxation.

Take into consideration every part of your life. Sign up for a pre-planned meal service to ensure that you'll always have something healthy on hand for busy workdays. Get a Fitbit to help you track how much you are moving, and start taking calls while going for walks. Perhaps most importantly, pencil plenty of time in your calendar for your family. Blocking out time in the morning and evening to spend with them will keep you grounded and help you remember what's really important in life.

Remember: Avoiding stress and burnout are essential to the long-term viability of your business.

Every part of your business has the potential to stress you out and keep you up at night—lack of sales, too much debt, not enough money, issues with employees, problems with equipment, and operations. Your brain will constantly be going. All your problems and thoughts will whirl around, making you tired and anxious. The pressure of constantly finding ways to grow your bottom line in business will build.

Creating and owning a business is stressful, and you can't really escape it. The sooner you learn stress management, the better. As an entrepreneur, you will know a lot about anxiety and stress. Here are some tips for combating stress:

Pay attention to your body's stress signals.

Typical signals of stress include sweating and an increased heart rate. It's important to recognize these signals and get them under control. This could involve simple, deep-breathing exercises.

Deal with the stress head on.

Rather than procrastinate, think about what is causing the emotional reaction and get a handle on it. Deal with the cause of stress right away, whether it's a phone call from an angry client or making a difficult business decision.

Take breaks.

When you feel stress coming on, get up and do something else such as taking a brief walk or going outside. This short break can give you a different perspective on a stressful situation and at least provide short-term relief from the physical effects of stress.

Adopt a healthy lifestyle.

Thirty minutes of vigorous exercise at least three times a week can help you reduce stress. Good eating habits such as including more fruits and vegetables in your diet can give you more energy and help you handle stress better.

Try to achieve work-life balance.

Although today's business environment can be demanding, it's crucial to take time for other activities outside of the office such as family events, hobbies, and sports. This is when you will recharge your batteries.

Keep perfectionism in check.

Offering a quality product and service doesn't mean obsessing about it. Know when to get a task off your desk and focus on doing your best in a competitive environment.

Delegate to reduce your workload.

Accept that you can't do it all. Rather than micro-managing, delegate responsibility to employees or contractors or hire a VA and leave him or her alone to do the job. Sharing the load can relieve stress.

Find people you trust and confide in them.

Talking to others about business issues can help you find solutions to deal with challenges. Entrepreneurs can also network with other people in their industries to see how they are handling similar issues.

Get your business' finances under control.

Cash flow is a major source of anxiety for entrepreneurs. Find ways to better monitor your revenue and expenses. Also, find ways to improve productivity and ultimately your company's financial health.

Commit to vacation time.

Give yourself time off to relax, particularly during challenging periods. For example, turn your phone off when you're on a holiday. Postponing a vacation may have short-term benefits for your business but in the long run, your health could suffer and cause greater problems down the road.

Rank your tasks.

One of the causes of stress in business is having so many things to work on that none of them get done. If you try to do a little bit of each task, you will complete few of them. Don't try to do everything at once. Try to focus on one or few tasks at a time.

You need to prioritize your goals. Write down everything that you need to complete. Then, rank your tasks from greatest to least important. The tasks you need to do first should be at the top of your list. As you work, focus on the most important tasks. Once you finish those, you can move down the list. You're essentially creating an agenda for yourself.

Now, some people might get stressed when they see the number of tasks they need to complete. Try not to get overwhelmed by the length of your list. Focus on what you need to work on next.

Take breaks.

This is probably the simplest piece of stress-relieving advice for business owners: take a break. If you're constantly spinning your wheels, not getting anywhere, and stressing about the problem, a short break might be all you need. Stepping away from the stressor for even ten minutes can refresh and calm you. Breaks can even prevent burnout.

When you take a break, do something that relaxes you. Go for a walk. Get some coffee. Call a friend. Watch a funny video. Don't do anything business related. When you get back to your business, you will have a clearer mind. You will have fresh energy to tackle the task. Stepping away might even open your eyes to a new and better way to complete the task.

Take care of yourself.

Good health is important when you're an entrepreneur. Running a business takes a lot out of you. Your small business comes with long nights, early mornings, no weekends, and no sick days. Your non-stop life puts strain on your body, and then you add stress on top of that.

You need to take care of yourself. Don't forget to do the simple things. Drink water throughout the day. Regularly eat. Get some sleep. Try to add in some additional self-care, too. Go to a health food store and buy some natural supplements. Reduce your caffeine consumption. When you're healthy, your body can better handle the stress.

If you can, exercise regularly. While exercise will make you physically fit, it is also a great method to manage stress as a small business owner. Through exercise, you can release your anxieties and frustrations. You can clear your mind and relax. Even a small amount of exercise can reduce your stress.

Remember what's going right.

As you're building your business, it is easy to only focus on what's going wrong. You can become stressed when you're looking at all the things that are behind schedule, underfunded or need to be fixed.

You can improve your stress management in business by reminding yourself of what's going right. List out all your accomplishments and any small business milestones you've achieved. There are probably more than you realize. Don't neglect even the smallest accomplishments. Put your list somewhere you can easily see it, such as on your desk or the wall. Whenever you feel stressed about everything going wrong, look at your list and add to it. Take a moment to remember all the jobs well done.

Last resort- PURGE your brain.

As a business owner, there's rarely a separation between work and home. You'll constantly think about your business and work you could be doing. Sometimes, you can't stop thinking about your business. Your brain is on nonstop, even when you're trying to sleep.

When my brain won't shut down, I write everything down that my mind is trying to process. I'll write down my problem, possible solutions, and miscellaneous notes. Sometimes writing all of your thoughts can take a while, but it's worth it. After I write everything down, I can relax and sleep. My brain doesn't have anything to process because I put all my thoughts in a safe place. I don't have to worry about my business for a time because I know everything is waiting for me later, and I don't have to worry about forgetting anything.

One of my favorite stress-relieving tactics is writing in a stress diary. You may already be doing the next steps, but maybe just sporadically. However, you choose, it will help alleviate your anxiety.

Many of us experience stress in some form every day, whether it's caused by rush-hour traffic, a heavy workload, difficult customers, or unpleasant news. The problem is that, if stress goes unchecked, it can affect our productivity and, worse still, our health.

This is where keeping a stress diary can be useful. Going through the process of logging anxious moments is good for understanding the causes of short-term stress in your life.

This is important because, often, these stressors flit in and out of our minds without getting the attention and focus that they deserve. A stress diary can give an insight into how you react to stress and help you to identify the levels of pressure at which you prefer to operate. (After all, a little bit of pressure can be a good thing!)

The idea behind stress diaries is that, on a regular basis, you record information about the stresses you're experiencing, so that you can analyze these stresses and then manage them. As well as helping you to capture and analyze the most common sources of stress in your life, stress diaries help you to understand:

- The causes of stress in more detail.

- The levels of pressure at which you operate most effectively.

- How you may be able to improve the way you manage stress.

To get started, if you don't have my Stress Diary Template, designate a specific notebook as your diary and make regular entries (for example, every hour).

(If you have any difficulty remembering to write in your stress diary, set an alarm to remind you to make your next entry.)

Make an entry in your diary after any stressful incidents, and record the following information:

- The date and time.

- The most recent stressful event you experienced.

- How happy you feel now, using a scale of one (the unhappiest you've ever been) to ten (the happiest you've been). As well as, write down the mood you're feeling.

- How effectively you're working now (on a scale of zero). A zero here would equal complete ineffectiveness, while a ten would show the greatest effectiveness you have ever achieved.

- The fundamental cause of the stress (be as honest and objective as possible).

You may also want to note:

- The symptoms you felt (for example, "butterflies in the stomach," anger, headache, raised pulse rate, sweaty palms, and so on).

- How well you handled the event: did your reaction help solve the problem, or did it make things worse?

Physician, heal yourself... Analyzing the Diary

Once you've kept a Stress Diary for a number of days, you can analyze it and act:

- First, look at the different stresses you experienced during the time you kept your diary. Highlight the most frequent stresses, and also the ones that were most unpleasant.

- Look at your assessments and their underlying causes, and your appraisal of how well you handled the stressful events. Do these highlight problems that need to be fixed? If so, list these areas.

- Next, look through your diary at the situations that cause you stress. List ways in which you can change these situations for the better.

- Finally, look at how you felt when you were under pressure, and explore how it affected your happiness and your effectiveness. Was there a middle level of pressure at which you were happiest and performed best?

Having analyzed your diary, you should fully understand what the most important and frequent sources of stress are in your life, and you should appreciate the levels of pressure at which you are happiest. You should also know the sort of situations that cause you stress, so that you can prepare for them and manage them well.

You'll reap the real benefits of having a stress diary in the first few weeks that you use it. After this, you may find that you have better uses for your time.

If, however, your lifestyle changes, or you begin to suffer from stress again, then it may be worth using the diary approach one more time. You'll probably find that the stresses you face have changed.

What's Next?

Your next step is to get your stress under control. Start by looking at the people and events that cause the most stress for you.

- Is there a person or group of people that cause your stress?

- Does any of your stress come from disorganization, lack of knowledge, or time-management?

- Is burnout contributing to the stress you're experiencing?

Some stresses will be unavoidable, especially if you're in a job with lots of responsibility. If this sounds like your situation, here's what you can do:

- Consider taking a vacation. Keep in mind that although the people or tasks that cause your stress will still be waiting for you when you return, a vacation can give you enough distance to relax, refresh, and come up with some effective solutions.

- Meditation can be very effective for dealing with stress, even if you can only meditate for five minutes at a time.

- Are you getting enough rest? Most people need seven-to-eight hours of sleep to stay healthy and productive. A lack of sleep can definitely contribute to your stress level. A lot of people are sleeping but not resting.

- Do you find it difficult to "switch off" at end of the day? Learn how to relax after a hard day.

Q-Tip #6: Warning...

Stress can cause severe health problems and, in extreme cases, death. While these management techniques can have a positive effect on reducing stress, they should be used for guidance only. Always take the advice of a qualified health professional if you have any concerns about stress-related illnesses.

Chapter 7:

MONEY MANAGEMENT

"The price of anything is the amount of life you exchange for it."
- Henry David Thoreau

Money Talk...Securing the Bag

How many times have you been told that saving money is a good thing? Everyone says to put a little on the side for a rainy day. Financial gurus recommend that you save a bit of money every month, but that's easier said than done. After all, it's not uncommon for people to live paycheck-to-paycheck. And that is especially true for entrepreneurs. We're going into business for our ourselves because our current outlook is bleak. But until we are making what we need to make, we continue to work a nine-to-five. The irony is that the same job that you have acknowledged doesn't pay you what you're worth, is the same job that now needs to fund your current lifestyle and invest in your dreams, at the same time.

So how can that work?

If you want to start a company, you'll need to start budgeting and saving. At times, this will feel impossible. But it must be done if you want you to invest in your future.

Here are a few ways to start managing your money more effectively:

1. Prioritize organization.

When you are organized, you can track every aspect of your finances. Record all of your financial information in one place so you can refer to it and keep track of your progress. You may want to try and organize it by category. For example, you can categorize items as "urgent" and "future." Or create finance envelopes. For instance, I keep an envelope in my car labeled transportation. I put all my gas and toll receipts inside. I also put my car repair receipts in there as well. When I need to review the finances, revisit my budget, or meet with the accountant, I know all the receipts are in a safe place, in one place.

2. Check your credit.

Know your credit score. It doesn't matter what shape it's in, you need to know. If it's great, it may open some doors for your business. If there's room for improvement, at least you will know what you need to focus on.

Understanding your credit score and improving it to the best of your ability is critical when it comes to money management. Not always, but often, the level of credit a new business receives is often dependent on the owner's personal credit score.

3. Save where you can.

People often cringe when they think about cutting back. Fortunately, there are several painless ways to save. Look at your daily habits and see if you have any spending trends. For example, if you spend six dollars every day on a Venti Vanilla White Mocha, you might consider cutting back and only having it on the weekends or perhaps every other day. Slowly, you'll get used to this new habit, and your bank account will reap the rewards. For me (yes that is my guilty pleasure) six dollars six days a week equals thirty-six dollars. In a month that's $144. And in a year, that's over $1,700. Now I'm not suggesting that I will never splurge on my favorite coffee drink. What I am saying is: what if I need new office equipment and my savings cannot cover it? An extra $1,700 could either cover this expense or at least put a dent in it. Imagine if you could designate two or three luxuries to put aside for now. Where would you be at the end of the year?

4. Set short-and long-term goals.

Have you ever noticed that people want to reach their goals in as little time as possible? Does that describe you? If you pick up almost any given health or beauty magazine, it'll claim that it can help you achieve extreme results in little-to-no time. Unfortunately, they lie! Crash diets are often ineffective, special "miracle" beverages don't melt your love handles away, and there is no such thing as "get rich quick."

It's sometimes hard to accept that your goals will take time to accomplish, which is why you should create short and long-term goals. In either case, aim to make goals that are specific, measurable, attainable, relevant, and time-based (S.M.A.R.T.). When you accomplish your short-term goals, you will receive the positive reinforcement that you need to forge toward your long-term goals.

5. Find a mentor.

Sometimes you just need help. Ask a professional if you feel it's too overwhelming. Financial planning can sometimes feel that way. You can seek out mentors who can help you with personal finances, budgeting, and forecasting.

After reading these tips, you may be wondering why the list of expenses you jot down in the Notes section of your cell phone isn't enough. After all, you're an up-and-coming business owner and you should really be making money not counting it.

Why is money management and budgeting important for you and your business? Glad you asked. There are many mistakes we could make when we don't have discipline in these areas:

1. We would live beyond our means. Often, what's in our head is not what's in the bank. We need to see what's coming in and going out. If the amounts do not gel, we need to make some changes. And actually, for any new entrepreneur, you should probably make these concessions anyway. And by new entrepreneur, I am referring to anyone who has not been able to leave a nine-to-five, has not realized a consistent profit, or hasn't reached a point where the business can at least pay for itself. And that's not a bad thing. That's just where you are in your business process or timeline. However, if you've been

"new" in practices and in results, but you've been in business for a while now, you should ask yourself if your lack of planning and budgeting has something to do with it.

"There is no dignity quite so impressive, and no independence
quite so important,
as living within your means."
- Calvin Coolidge

Budgeting

The first step to any solid personal finance plan is budgeting. You cannot wing it. You will inevitably miss something. One of the easiest and most basic approaches is to subtract your expenses from your income. Whatever is leftover is considered discretionary.

However, for entrepreneurs, that still doesn't cut it. You now have a new and quite substantial investment for which you are responsible. If you don't plan for it, you may wind up putting it on the side whenever money's low. A budget will help you start your business and establish a customized plan for how fast you can move forward.

Emergency Funds

Are you prepared for summer vacations or an awful winter Nor'easter? What happens if you go through a tough period, a dry spell, and you can't turn a profit? Obviously, this is not the goal. But as the saying goes, it's better to be safe than sorry. You should have an emergency fund for both your personal and business finances. This may sound like a nightmare, but it's only a nightmare if you're not prepared. A responsible entrepreneur is prepared. If you don't already have an emergency fund established, you should set aside a little bit of money every month until you've reached your desired goal.

Reduce Your Debt

Debt can be problematic for entrepreneurs. Don't they say you have to go into debt to make money? So, what happens after you've acquired this debt? You could possibly be paying the interest on debts, loans, credit cards, etc. consistently, for a while.

While you can't eliminate some debt, it's in your best interest to eliminate the gravy off of your budget. There are certain debts that could be categorized as luxuries or wants. While you're paying down your investments, try to eliminate some of these debts. Once you reduce and payoff some debt, you can add a few of these back if you'd like. But I think you'll be surprised at how you won't miss certain things once they're gone.

> *"The speed of your success is limited only by your dedication and what you're willing to sacrifice"*
> ***- Nathan W. Morris***

So, what's next? Can all this money talk be simplified? Yes. Here are some do's and don'ts to start you along the way.

DON'T…

DON'T freak out when the money fluctuates.

No matter how much you plan and save, there will be periods of time when income fluctuates. Don't freak out. Whether we admit it or not, it has happened to everyone. Entrepreneurship means not shutting your doors even if the business is a little slow.

DON'T overspend and call it an investment.

Overspending will create unnecessary debt for your business. It will end up feeling like you have a j-o-b because you will find yourself simply working paycheck-to-paycheck to keep your business afloat and bills paid, including the debt.

DO…

DO have a budget.

If we're being honest, you actually need two budgets – one for the business and one for personal. You've got to understand personal finances in order to create a business budget that fits your lifestyle. Create a list of all monthly income and expenses. This includes mortgage or rent, car payments, credit cards and other loans, utilities, savings contributions, child expenses, and other bills. This total is the minimum your business needs to pay you in order to maintain the lifestyle to which you've become accustomed.

DO invest in yourself and your business.

One of the greatest gifts you can give yourself as an entrepreneur is the gift of personal development. Until you're willing to invest in yourself, your business can only go but so far.

DO create policies and procedures.

Sounds crazy that you'd need to have a procedure in place if you're an entrepreneur but without it, you are likely wasting time and money.

Q-Tip #7: Create separate budgets and accounts for personal and business expenses and hire help to save money in the long run.

Chapter 8:

THE POWER OF THE FOLLOW-UP

"The fortune is in the follow-up."

It's become an old saying for good reason. Because it's true. Following up with customers and clients can be one of THE most important business actions an entrepreneur can take. It is an essential key to success that, once mastered, will bring awesome results.

The problem is people don't *like* doing follow-ups. There's so much resistance to the idea of following up because most are so terrified.

I understand that people are afraid to come off as pushy in their follow-ups. However, I'm about to explain why that logic doesn't even make sense and that you just need to get over it. Here's why.

People are busy.

Do you have any idea how many things are vying for people's attention in their inboxes? A lot. The chances of your email getting lost or forgotten under a massive pile of other emails is pretty high.

Additionally, life happens, and people are busy. Not everyone is on top of their email game like you may be. Not only that, but what if they were traveling or got sick? All of these things could lead to someone not responding to you which is why follow ups are so important.

Case and point. I was hired to update a client's books and do some light accounting work for him. I noticed that the more I entered his invoices, over eighty percent had not been paid. This was no longer a simple data entry project. So, I began to call these customers, most who had already received several visits and services rendered, to request payment. Overwhelmingly, the response I received was, "Great! I've been waiting for *you* to contact *me*. I knew I owed money, just didn't know how much..." and more of the like.

They were waiting for *us*!

Amazing right? Every now and then, you will have a customer call you to make sure you receive payment. But more than likely, they will wait for you.

People need to hear from you an average of seven times.

Another reason why follow ups are so important is because people will need to hear from you an average of seven times before they finally decide to purchase something from you. That's right. *Seven.*

That means that sending an email <u>once</u> is not enough. It also means that if someone does not respond the first time, it doesn't necessarily mean he or she is not interested. Like I said, maybe this person is just busy. Or, maybe they just haven't heard from you enough yet, which is why you need to remain consistent with follow-ups. People may observe you to see just how bad you want their business.

You really are leaving money on the table.

I already gave a clear-cut example of how it took months of consistent follow-up for a client to finally see big results. Had I not done this, he would have lost out on even more money.

The data doesn't lie.

(Take a look at these statistics by Hubport.)

- **Eighty percent** of sales require five follow-up phone calls after the meeting.

- **Thirty-five to fifty percent** of sales go to the vendor that responds first.
- When companies follow up on web leads within five minutes, they are **nine** times more likely to convert potential customers.
- **Sixty-three percent** of people requesting info on your company today won't purchase for at least three months.
- **Twenty percent** will take more than twelve months to buy.
- **Fifty percent** of leads are qualified but not yet ready to buy.
- **Ninety-three percent** of converted leads are contacted by the sixth call attempt.

As you can see, follow-ups are a necessary part of the sales process. There is absolutely no way around this fact and the numbers do not lie. And for those thinking, "Well this doesn't apply to me because I'm not *in* sales" …. I beg to differ. If you're an entrepreneur, you *are* in sales. You're selling an idea, a concept, a book, a service, or even a craft. And these statistics pertain to you.

It's easier than ever to create consistent follow-ups.

With all the tools available at your disposal these days, follow ups don't need to take a whole lot of time. To name a few, here are some of the ways to either automate or delegate follow-ups in your business so to ensure they are getting done without wasting time.

○ Automated email marketing after a presentation.

○ Create a weekly blog that is sent out via email.

○ Automated emails after a consultation call that are tailored to the specific needs of your clients.

○ Delegate manual email follow-ups to your assistant or VA (Virtual Assistant).

○ Create follow-up templates to use and tweak depending on the lead.

○ Use tools like Microsoft Outlook or Streak for Gmail to schedule manual follow-ups in advance.

Like I said, there are tons of ways to make sure your follow-ups are getting done. The hardest part is creating the content and getting everything situated in your email marketing system. Once that's done, it all runs automatically without you having to touch it and it's very effective.

Consistent follow-ups will put you ahead of the game.

One last astonishing statistic… **forty-four percent** of salespeople give up after one follow up.

How much money are you leaving on the table? This means that if you stay consistent with your follow-ups, you're already ahead of half the people with whom you may be competing.

The more you follow up, the more you increase your chances of making money. Once you realize that follow-ups are an important part of making money in your business, you won't make the mistake of leaving money on the table because you're too afraid to follow up.

Eight reasons to follow-up

If the statistics above weren't enough to convince you that the fortune is in the follow-up, here are eight more reasons why you must create a system for connecting with potential customers after your initial touch.

1. When customer expectations are fulfilled, they will have more reasons to purchase from you.

Customers stick with your business for a longer period of time if you are always available. They remember you for the rest of their lives for delivering great customer service. "Follow-up" is a synonym for customer service. That being said, there's a high possibility that your brand might spread among other people without you even knowing about it. Easy marketing.

2. Follow-ups make customers feel special and therefore this increases your reliability and relatability "points" with your customers.

3. A regular follow-up always gives customers a chance to be heard and engage effectively.

4. Follow-ups can be a great opportunity to ask customers what they want or expect next.

5. Customers usually want a customized path to get in touch with the company. Therefore, the follow-up system enhances this type of communication.

6. A follow-up call should always be implemented after conducting a marketing campaign or attending a networking event. Follow-up with everyone, including those who just inquired or expressed an interest in your products or services. You might just get a lead! If you don't have time, delegate these tasks to a VA.

7. Existing customers who receive follow ups are more likely to take advantage of the new product than people who don't receive follow-ups.

8. Did you know that eighty percent of sales are secured between the fifth and twelfth contacts with ideal prospects?

What does that mean for your service-based business? It means you're losing sales every day due to poor follow-up.

Here's a scary reality: the average salesperson only makes two attempts to reach a prospect!

But look at this breakdown of a sale closed:

- Two percent of sales are made on the first contact.
- Three percent of sales are made on the second contact.
- Five percent of sales are made on the third contact.
- Ten percent of sales are made on the fourth contact.
- Eighty percent of sales are made on the fifth to twelfth contacts.

Can you see room for improvement in your follow-up process?

Here are three follow-up strategies:

1. Be consistent.

After an initial call you might get discouraged because you didn't close the client on the spot. Resist the tendency to get irritated when you don't see results right away.

Knowing your end goal is the key.

Start by knowing your numbers. How many clients do you need to have each month to reach your revenue goal? What's your conversion rate? How many people do you need to speak with in order to secure those clients? Create a system that allows you to track your sales calls, take follow-up notes, review all leads once a week, and then follow-up.

2. Provide value.

Why do your clients buy from you?

Because you are a solution to their problems. You are adding value to their lives.

During your sales and follow-up process, you need to show your client that you are the solution for them by adding value. Providing value before they give you a dime makes it about them and not about you.

- Share resources.
- Provide links to articles or blog posts that would help solve a problem they mentioned.
- Connect them to people who can help them grow their businesses.
- Send them a tool you have that may possibly move them closer to a "yes" in working with you.

3. Give social proof.

People like stories. If you've seen someone's journey online and looked at their business strategy and read about their plan and saw their results, you are much more apt to try what they are selling than if someone just *tells* you what they did. Show the proof!

Send a testimonial to a potential client so they can see themselves on the other side of working with you. If people can relate to your clients, they can relate to you, and understand the value of working with you.

Here's one thing you must ALWAYS do...

During your first call, get your next call or meeting scheduled.

I like to send action steps to my ideal clients after the call, this gives them a taste of what it will be like to work together. It also helps them look forward to our next interaction. They start thinking of the questions they may have for me, ideas they want to share, services they may need from me. Whatever the case, they're more likely to keep our next appointment.

There's no question about the power of follow-up. If you act on one or all of these three strategies, you'll have more business than you know what to do with.

Success = Ideas + Follow-up

When someone introduces me to an "idea person," I automatically jump to the conclusion that this person doesn't do follow-up because they're the "creative" on the team. Of course, there are people who are great at getting things done but haven't had an original idea in their lives. Great entrepreneurs, like Bill Gates, are great at both.

That's how you should aspire to be. I can think of several important principles for starting and running a business. And for each principle, follow-up, or lack of it, can make or break the startup.

Here are a few:

Business networking. For entrepreneurs, effective networking is required to find investors, partners, and customers. It doesn't work if you don't follow up on networking opportunities, networking referrals, and ongoing networking relationships.

Investor negotiations. Serious investors expect owners to have their homework done before the first interaction - a documented executive summary, business plan, and financial model. They expect prompt formal follow-up to questions. Too many entrepreneurs try to talk their way through all of these.

THE QUINTESSENTIAL GUIDE FOR ENTREPRENEURS

Product development. For a great idea person, the product details keep changing for the better, but nothing ever gets finished. Lists of project milestones and technical issues are created, but nothing happens on time, because follow-up on issues is missing.

Time management. Some struggling entrepreneurs are totally event driven. They are too busy with the "crisis of the moment" to focus on follow-ups that may save a major customer, close a partner deal, or solidify a process that isn't working well.

Effective marketing. Guerrilla marketing stresses the importance of prospect follow-up if you even hope to succeed in business. If you collect business cards at a trade show, make sure you follow-up with them all within seventy-two hours, and at least three more times after that.

Customer retention. More customers are lost to apathy after the sale than poor service or quality. Many experts suggest it costs six times more to sell something to a new customer than to an existing customer. A numbing **sixty-eight percent** of all business lost in America is lost due to a lack of follow-up after the sale. WOW!

Professional relationships. How many people do you know who have a thousand emails in their inboxes, or just a few awaiting follow-up for over a week from people who matter? Procrastination jeopardizes your integrity and your relationships. Everyone likes to be the one pursued rather than the pursuer. There's a reason that many people say that the fortune is in the follow up. When you follow up properly with people, your reputation will benefit, your business will benefit, and eventually your bank account will benefit as well.

Sidebar here… If you don't *do* follow-up, as I have often heard from entrepreneurs who feel that their job is to develop ideas and concepts only, I would suggest that you never aspire to be an entrepreneur, or a manager, or an executive for that matter. You won't be happy, and you won't do a good job, because that's what these leaders do most of the time. The idea time for most executives are in the shower or during other "off hours."

So, which is the most important, the idea or the follow-up? If you intend to be a great entrepreneur, you need both.

The Art of the Follow-up: Work Your Leads

Given how important good selling techniques are to driving revenues, I am shocked at how many entrepreneurs and salespeople are just bad at working their leads. This includes things like not following up on leads (or following up too much) and not knowing how to break down barriers, to get the lead to actually listen to a pitch.

Contact the right person in the first place.

If somebody is not getting back to you, often times it is because he or she is the wrong person in the organization to make decisions about your product or service. Therefore, before you even send out your first outreach package, make sure the person you are reaching out to has decision-making control for your solution. For example, if you are selling a social media management software, it is most likely the head of social media communications at that company—not social media advertising, not their head of marketing, not their CEO, etc. who will decide if they want to hire you. If you are unclear who is the right person, ask to be pointed in the right direction, or send messages to all logical candidates until you find the right person with whom to engage.

Make good first impressions.

Another reason people don't get back to you is they don't like what you have to say. Often times people are so excited about the "what" they are selling, that they don't focus on the more important benefits of "why" a customer would want to buy it.

Simplify your pitch so that you are helping them understand you are selling a need-to-have "painkiller" for their problems, not a nice-to-have "vitamin." Be solutions-driven. As an example, for the social media management software, it is less about how it integrates with Facebook and Twitter for easy communications (blah, blah, blah), and more about how it will help them double their base of social media followers and help them generate more revenue. So, put on their hat, not yours, to figure out what would resonate most with them.

Follow-up in the right frequency and format.

It shocks me how many times people forget to follow up with their old leads. I live by the three-strike rule within a once-per-week follow-up schedule. So, for example, if you first email them on March 1st, your first follow-up will be on March 8th, and your second follow up with be on March 16th. If they don't get back to you after three tries, it is time to move on, but don't forget about them. Put them into a long-term "nurturing" schedule, sending along interesting research or insights that show them you are well informed on their needs and interests, for them to want to engage with you in the future. Then you can restart a more direct selling effort again in the following quarter.

Shake up the methods in which you make your outreach.

Email is easy and can be automated. But, it is a lot less personable than a phone call, where they can better hear your voice and personality shine through. And, you never know, you may call, and they just might actually pick up their phones. This is particularly effective during the 8-9 a.m. or 5-6 p.m. timeframes, while they are most likely in the office, but their assistants are away.

Shake up your messaging.

You can only browbeat a person so many times with the same message before it falls on deaf ears. You may need to shake up your messaging. Start with an introduction about your business and its benefits to them. If that doesn't work, send them some interesting market research. If that doesn't work, invite them as your guest to some key industry event. And, if all else fails, everybody loves a free lunch, golf invitation, or tickets to the ballgame. An unexpected gift sent to their office also works well (obviously within reason and appropriate with what you ask - don't do too much or it'll come across as creepy), and they will hopefully call to say, "thank you." Do whatever you need to do to get them on the phone or to a meeting to hear what you have to say. Persistence without being annoying is the key here.

Break down barriers.

It also surprises me that when a salesperson hits a wall, they stop trying, instead of tearing down that wall. For example, if a target lead is not responding to you, try to develop a relationship with the assistant or coworkers. The executive assistant is usually THE person to actually speak to. Executive assistants handle calendars. They can move meetings around and move others to the top.

If you hit a dead end with one person in the department, start again with another person in a different department. For example, if the Chief Marketing Officer (CMO) won't listen to your pitch, try calling his or her Chief Financial Officer (CFO) to talk about the cost savings your product could provide, so the CFO can help you get the attention of the CMO. There is no such thing as a dead end—keep trying until someone gives you a chance.

Frustrated. Annoyed. Ignored. These are the feelings you may have felt the last time you phoned or sent out an email or text and never received a response.

It's extremely irritating when a request goes unanswered. How do you follow-up without being a pest? There could be multiple reasons why you did not receive a response. Perhaps the recipient didn't see your message, or got too busy to respond right away, or saw it and forgot to answer…the list goes on.

Here are some guidelines for following up.

1. Always assume the best.

Don't take it personal. More than likely, there is a good reason why the recipient hasn't answered. Nevertheless, let the person know that you are waiting for a response, especially if you have a deadline. You might write something like, "I hope you received my email. I haven't heard back so I wanted to follow up on my previous message."

Quench the instinct to lash out with anger or accusations as in, "It's been five days. Why haven't you responded?"

Give the recipient the benefit of the doubt. I remember being frustrated by suddenly not hearing back from a colleague after a flurry of emails. When she finally got back in touch, it turned out she had been called away to care for a sick parent and simply didn't have the energy left to devote to our program at that time. We reconnected in four months and started our work plan together.

Life happens so try to be understanding.

2. Give the recipient an easy "opt-out."

Sometimes you just need to know if it's time to move on (for now). If you have not received a response despite your follow-up efforts, kindly let the person off the hook. One time a client asked me to send him a proposal. After I did not hear back from him in three weeks. I wrote, "Please let me know if you would still like for me to hold the date for your program that we discussed. If I don't hear back from you, I'll go ahead and close your file."

Almost instantly, I heard back with a kind, "Thank you, but we've decided not to proceed with the program at this time." Disappointed? Yes. But at least I had an answer for the immediate future. It also opened up a door for me to ask questions and circle back with a better option for that customer.

You can also write something like, "I know you're busy, so I don't want to keep contacting you if you have decided to move in a different direction or if you have selected another vendor. When you're ready to reach out again, please do. I'd be happy to resume our conversation."

3. Appeal to a person's passion.

A manager can receive an average of 121 emails per day. One way to break through the clutter is by mentioning a person's passion. The next time you follow up, mention something that you both have in common. For example, if the person is a football fan, mention the latest football game. If they like to travel, share a story about their or your latest trip. You can often learn a person's interests through their Facebook or LinkedIn profiles, through their company website or blog, or just by talking to them directly. If there was a specific topic that you bonded over during your last call, this is the time to mention it. Remind them of the initial connection you made.

4. Make contact at different times of the day.

Vary the times of day you correspond and see if one time of day is better than another for receiving responses. Most important people start their days very early and end their days late after everyone has left the office.

Q-Tip #8: Create an intentional plan for how you will follow-up with leads, and schedule that time on your calendar each week.

Chapter 9:

REJECTION: HOW TO HANDLE THE NO'S AND KEEP IT MOVING

"Success is the ability to go from failure to failure without a loss of enthusiasm."
- Winston Churchill

How hard is it for you to deal with rejection? For many, consistent rejection can crush confidence. If you're anything like I was when I first started out, you're probably finding it incredibly difficult.

If you have experienced a lot of rejection, you have probably felt discouraged and frustrated. As a matter of fact, you may have even felt tempted to give up.

Don't worry, that's normal.

There is good news. Rejection doesn't have to paralyze you. It doesn't have to keep you from moving forward. We all deal with rejection at some point, but it's never fun to deal with rejection in your business.

The way you handle rejection can make a big difference in your business and your life down the road. When you are rejected, it can feel like a blow to your self-esteem — and even to your dreams. If you give in to those feelings, you can lose your way.

Instead, learn to handle rejection in your business, and you will be more likely to thrive in the long run. Here are some tips that can help you:

1. Acknowledge your disappointment.

The first thing to do is acknowledge your feelings and your disappointment. Everyone feels bad when they've been rejected. Whether your application for a small business loan was turned down or a potential partner backed out of a deal, it stings.

Pretending it doesn't hurt won't help anyone. Face your emotions head-on and figure out how you can move forward. It will help you improve your mental strength. Plus, it will keep you from going down a road in which you bottle everything up, causing bigger problems later.

2. Find the lesson.

Next, find the lesson in the rejection. Usually, there's something you can learn from the experience. Maybe you didn't have a strong business plan, so an investor decided to pull back. Perhaps you made a mistake in the way you handled a problem. In some cases, you might experience rejection in your business because you just haven't grown enough.

Whatever the reason for the rejection, it's important to look for ways to improve. Don't use the rejection as a reason to quit. Instead, look at it as a chance to improve. Make some tweaks. Maybe you even need to start from scratch. But take the lesson and apply it so your next attempt isn't as likely to fail.

3. Be kind to yourself.

It's not uncommon for rejection in your business to lead to negative self-talk. Don't get caught in this trap. While you need to acknowledge weaknesses and conditions that could be improved, rejection doesn't mean that you are down for the count.

Look for ways to introduce more affirming self-talk so that you can move forward. Be kind to yourself. Don't keep beating yourself up. We all make mistakes. We're all rejected. And sometimes that rejection has more to do with external factors than internal factors.

Allow yourself some grace, pick yourself up, and then try again.

4. Don't let rejection in your business define you.

If your family doesn't support your business, or if an investor decides not to provide you with funds, don't let that define you as unsuccessful. In fact, don't take it as a sign of anything other than it wasn't the right opportunity.

You're only unsuccessful if you give up! Plenty of successful entrepreneurs had setbacks and experienced rejection. Rejection is a sign you've put yourself out there. You can't succeed if you don't take a few risks.

You don't need to let rejection get you down. Sure, give yourself time to process the disappointment for one day. However, once you're done with your short pity party, it's time to get back to work building that successful business.

Principles for Handling Rejection

1. Adopt a position of buoyancy.

When I think of buoyancy, I think of the toy clown my cousins had when we were growing up. It was weighted at the bottom and we treated it as punching bags of sorts. We would hit it, it would go down, and immediately pop back up. I believe this is the exact quality that helps entrepreneurs continue to persevere even in the face of constant rejection. Take a "no" and rebound quickly. Success requires you to keep going even if you hear the word "no" over and over again. You have to be mentally tough.

One of the key factors of buoyancy is inquisitive self-talk. Instead of just telling yourself that you can make the sale, ask yourself if you can make the sale. You're not saying, "I can do this." You're saying, "Can I do this?" While this may seem counter-productive, analytical self-talk is actually more effective.

The reason it's more effective is because framing your self-talk as questions will demand you to think of answers. In order to answer the question you're asking yourself, you will begin formulating the strategy you will use. This increases the odds that you will succeed.

2. Implement a posture of confidence.

One of the negative effects of rejection in business is that it can slowly eat away at your confidence. This can cause serious setbacks when you have to make other attempts to influence.

When rejection threatens to rob you of your confidence, you must act. Literally. This is where your confidence posture comes in. Confidence posture consists of movements and poses that communicate confidence and charisma.

Body language is EVERYTHING! It can actually influence the way you feel and how you see yourself. When you adopt a confident posture, you will begin to feel more confident.

The great thing about this is that it's so easy. You don't need anything special to do it. Just take ten-to-fifteen minutes and practice your confidence poses and you will begin to ease the sting of rejection. As a matter of fact, if you try this before you actually have to influence someone, it may decrease your chances of getting rejected in the first place!

3. Get a support system.

When you're starting your own business, you need all the support you can get. Being an entrepreneur is already stressful and emotionally taxing.

When you add constant rejection to that equation, it makes it much harder to maintain the attitude that you need to have in order to stay motivated. To combat this, you need people in your life that will push you to persevere even when you feel like a gigantic failure.

This means you need to avoid the naysayers! These are the people who want you to be "realistic" about your dreams and goals. They may believe they're doing you a favor, but they're actually becoming "confidence vacuums" that are sucking the motivation and confidence out of you.

Don't surround yourself with negative people. Try to stay away from them as much as you can. If you know other entrepreneurs, it's best to rely on them for the support you need. If you don't already know other entrepreneurs, try looking online for networking groups that cater to entrepreneurs.

4. Don't take it personal.

I've mentioned this before, but it's worth repeating, especially in this topic of rejection. "It's not personal, it's business." That's the attitude you need to have when you're faced with rejection in business.

If your prospect says "no," they're not rejecting you personally, they're rejecting your offer. I know that you may think your product or service is a part of you, but it's not. Not to your prospect.

Instead, think of it from a business perspective. Maybe they genuinely don't need what you have to offer. Maybe they really can't afford the price. If this is the case, then it's better that they say "no" rather than lead you on, right?

Of course, it's possible that they may be rejecting your offer because they think they don't need it or can't afford it. Maybe they're wrong. If this is the case, then it's up to you to show them the error of their ways! Make them an offer they can't refuse.

This brings me to my next point…

5. Rejection in business isn't always permanent.

The word "no" isn't always a no forever. You shouldn't give up just because your prospective customer or client isn't jumping on your offer right now. The conversation doesn't have to be over after a rejection. It's possible that it just isn't the right time.

Instead of throwing in the towel, try to find out what is needed to get to a "yes." Maybe the prospect just needs more time. Maybe there's a hidden objection that you need to uncover.

Regardless of the situation, your job as a salesperson is to find out what conditions are necessary for the prospect to accept your offer. This can be done by asking good questions and being patient.

I can't begin to count the opportunities that have come my way after I received an initial no. There were times I would receive a "Dear John" email stating that I didn't get the job or contract. There were definitely times I was disappointed, even COUNTING on the yes. But I resisted my feelings, and wrote back, thanking them for their time. I often said, "If anything changes, or the contract/employee doesn't work out, please reconsider me." There were so many companies that responded to me from that. I think they couldn't believe how honest and transparent I was being. And guess what? Many did call back!

It was worth the risk…

6. Identify opportunities for improvement.

One fact that will make you feel better about rejection is the idea that you are in control of the situation. Instead of just assuming that the decision was beyond your control, try to identify areas where you could have approached the situation better.

Chances are, there are some things you could have done to gain a more favorable result. Perhaps you didn't ask the right questions. Or maybe you didn't anticipate the objections.

Figure out what you could have done better, and it will increase the chances that you will get the sale next time. This can greatly improve your confidence.

7. Listen carefully (learn why you were rejected).

Don't just take the rejection at face value. If you earned the right to make your pitch, then you've earned the right to know why the prospect said "no."

If the client isn't ready to take the action you desire, then find out why. Sometimes, it may be beneficial to take the direct approach and ask what is keeping the company from accepting your offer. Listen carefully to what is being said so that you can figure out your next step in the process.

When you know the real reasons why you were rejected, it will be easier for you to take the right steps the next time around. This will make you feel better about the rejection and more likely to win the sale next time. But do it gently. You don't want to appear too aggressive or argumentative. That will burn a bridge for sure. Ask for feedback and most are willing to do just that.

8. Remember your victories.

One way to remain mentally tough is to remember the times you have succeeded. Instead of only focusing on the rejection, focus on the times when your potential clients said "yes."

There's something you must understand when you are attempting to influence others or their decisions: rejection is a part of business. You can't avoid it, but you can make it easier to deal with.

When you focus on your victories, it enables you to put things into perspective. The fact that you were rejected this time doesn't mean you won't be able to get anyone else to say yes. This is why it helps to think of times when you succeeded. It helps you stay motivated.

9. Get rejected!

The best way to become immune to the effects of rejection is to get rejected! If rejection is something that scares you, you can conquer this fear by facing it.

The more you get rejected, the easier it will get and the more you will learn. There have been people who have desensitized themselves to rejection by exposing themselves to it. In this way, you can keep rejection from discouraging you. It will no longer impact your psyche.

You want to be able to deal with rejection? Get rejected.

10. Find your groove.

Your groove, your vibe, your alter-ego, whatever you choose to call it, I'm talking about that quality that empowers you to keep going regardless of failure, setbacks, and challenges. It keeps you motivated even if you hear the word "no" over and over again. You will learn from your rejections and continue to improve.

You can be one of two types of people:

a. A person who assumes that their abilities and skills are set in stone and unable to move past their current skill level no matter how hard they work.

b. A person with a growth mindset, who understands that the only way to have true success is to be willing to dig deep and work for it. A growth-minded person puts in the work necessary to attain the level of success he or she desires.

Be a growth-minded entrepreneur. It will make you more influential.

Soon, rejection won't even phase you.

Turn it Around. Five ways you can turn that "NO" into a "YES"

1. Get a clue. "No" doesn't always mean no. Instead, often, it's just an easier answer than, "I'm not sure," or "I don't know," or "I'm not ready at this moment to give you an answer."

So, your first step is to be able to ascertain whether a "no" is really just a way to buy some time. Small business owners with whom you deal often resort to saying "no" because it saves time and is simply easier.

Lesson: "No" does not always mean "no."

2. It's not you, it's me. If you hear "no" a lot—too much—it is probably a hint that you are doing something wrong. The challenge then is to zero in on what that is. It could be any number of items:

Your pitch may be off, or too long, or not detailed enough. Your product could be too expensive, or may be too mediocre. Maybe your offer has no compelling call-to-action.

The best way to figure this out is to share what you are doing with a trusted colleague or mentor. Don't try and figure it out in a vacuum, because that obviously has not worked given the market feedback you have received.

Get some constructive criticism. Feedback is important; learn from it, change things up, and get back out there.

3. Deal with the objections. Zig Ziglar once said, "Every sale has five basic obstacles: no need, no money, no hurry, no desire, no trust."

That is a lot of no's, a lot of potential objections. But by understanding that "no" may really mean a prospect is actually worried about some or all of Ziglar's objections, you'll be armed with the ability to handle those doubts. If you forthrightly deal with their fears or objections, whatever they may be, then a no will not necessarily be their "final answer."

4. Make it better. I saw *Chicken Soup for the Soul* author Jack Canfield in an interview recently. Canfield shared a principle that he uses to turn a "maybe" or "no" into yes. He calls it "10." After he gives a pitch or proposal, he asks his potential customers, "Was my proposal a ten? If not, what would it take to make it a ten for you?"

Considering that *Chicken Soup for the Soul* book series sold over 250 titles with more than 110 million copies in the U.S. and Canada, translated into forty-three languages and sold more than 500 million worldwide, with product sales in excess of $2 billion, I think his advice is worth imitating. These stats are courtesy www.chicken-soup.com.

5. Don't take it too seriously. Having the right attitude about a no can really go a long way toward getting more 'yeses.' After all, what is a no except a prelude to the next yes? As long as you keep throwing your best pitches against the wall, something is bound to stick.

Always remember that Babe Ruth was not only the home run king, but also a leader in strikeouts. There's a good lesson for all of us in that.

And lastly,

Hearing no is NECESSARY to get to yes. Successful entrepreneurs understand that hearing no is part of getting to yes. They do not let every nuance of the word "no" strike them like arrows and deflate the rest of their sales presentations. Think about how the following comments by potential clients make you feel:

"Well, Raquel, that proposal you showed me sure is nice, but unfortunately, I'm just going to have to say, 'no.'"

"We appreciate all the information you've shared with us, Bob, but we're not going to do this right now."

Those are typical words and phrases entrepreneurs hear all day long, every day. For average people, those words signal defeat. The gut reaction experienced when hearing them is an immediate one—of failure and rejection—something people go through on a regular basis. Did you notice that I wrote "average"? Note: you are no longer average. Answering the call to be an entrepreneur, day in and day out sets you far apart from many others.

In fact, since rejections are so common, it's a wonder that so few entrepreneurs anticipate hearing them and prepare to deflect the negative feelings rejection can create. Most just accept those words and the feelings they generate as part of the game.

How often you hear the words and phrases like those above will depend on your abilities and skill. You need tenacity and resilience. What you do and say after hearing them will make a world of difference in your closing ratio and in your personal bottom line.

Getting to "Yes"

The starting point is "no."

The truth of the matter is that very few buyers will say "yes" the first time they're asked to purchase a product or service. Yet, the irony is that most people are willing to give up and accept rejection after hearing that first "no."

Think about how you would feel if you heard "no" over and over. If someone told you that in order to live a life you love or do more of it, you would be rejected and told "no" a lot, would you 1. keep pursuing your passion, or 2. reconsider this path altogether?

Would you feel the physical effect of disappointment? Would that sinking, let down feeling overcome you? It can be a tired feeling as your formerly pumped-up selling endorphins trickle down the drain.

If you were told "no" during an in-person pitch with a prospective client, would you mentally stop attempting to close the deal and simply move into, "Let's keep in touch" mode where you decide what to leave behind, what to pack away, and how to keep it together for your next meeting?

Would you say, "That's okay." "I understand." Or, "I'll touch back just in case you change your mind?" That's how average people respond.

My question to you today is this: Do you want to be average – or do you want to encourage yourself to become better than that? There's a whole lot to be done after you hear the word no. It's just a matter of understanding its many meanings, selecting the one this particular client means, and working with it.

When you understand that "no" doesn't always mean "no sale," those words will roll off your back like a duck sheds water and you'll keep paddling forward in the sales process.

"Making your mark on the world is hard. If it were easy, everybody would do it. But it's not. It takes patience, it takes commitment, and it comes with plenty of failure along the way."
- Barak Obama

Entrepreneurship is encompassed with rejection and failure. Being unsuccessful is part of the journey to success. To truly thrive as an entrepreneur and to stand out in your career you are going to need to take risks. Part of risk-taking is facing failure.

In a 2010 interview with Oprah, J.K Rowling said: "Failure is so important. We speak about success all the time. It is the ability to resist failure or use failure that often leads to greater success. I've met people who don't want to try for fear of failing."

Rowling is the epitome of success; her *Harry Potter* books are a sensation that inspired movies, video games, and theme parks. Can you imagine if her fear of failing stopped her from writing about a boy with a wand?

By embracing failure, you get to use it as a device to succeed. This doesn't mean pretending that failure isn't an option. It means that you aim to succeed in spite of the reality of failure.

It can inspire nonstop dedication to success. You should also use your failures, let them be lessons that keep you committed to your path.

Entrepreneurs hardly—if ever—get it right on the first try. If you instantly give up because you didn't succeed immediately, you will probably never succeed. But if you choose to learn from this, your mistakes and hardships can start to serve you.

Don't be discouraged, you're in good company...

Walt Disney was fired from the *Kansas City Star* in 1919, because his editor said, he "lacked imagination and had no good ideas."

While a junior fashion editor at *Harper's Bazaar*, Anna Wintour did lots of shoots, but apparently Tony Mazalla thought they were too edgy, and so she got fired after nine months, at which time, she became the fashion editor at *Viva*.

Oprah Winfrey was an evening news reporter and apparently got fired because she couldn't sever her emotions from her stories. Eventually, she was fired from Baltimore's WJZ-TV.

Albert Einstein didn't speak until he was four-years-old and didn't read until he was seven. He was subsequently expelled from school and was not admitted to the Zurich Polytechnic School. But eventually, he came around.

When President Abraham Lincoln was young and entered war, he entered as a captain, but came back as a much lower private. Later on, he tried to start a ton of businesses, all of which failed, and before becoming president, he lost several runs for public office.

Stephen King's most renowned and first book, *Carrie*, was rejected thirty times. King decided to toss the book, but his wife then went through the trash to rescue it and convinced him to re-submit it.

Michael Jordan was cut from his high school basketball team. He once said, "I have missed over 9,000 shots in my career. I have lost almost 300 games. On twenty-six occasions I have been entrusted to take the game-winning shot, and I have missed. I have failed over and over and over again in my life. And that is why I succeed."

If you've done everything you need to do, and they still say no, you still must keep it moving!

Q-Tip #9: Once you realize that some failure is inevitable, you will create a fail-proof environment.

Chapter 10:

HIRE A VIRTUAL ASSISTANT WHILE YOU STILL HAVE TIME!

One day, I was creating a list of benefits of being an entrepreneur, and I came across an article on *Entrepreneur* website. The writers do a great job at explaining why building a life you love as an entrepreneur is a good idea. Check out an excerpt from the article below:

1. You can be a workaholic if you want to.

Workaholics get a bad rap for all the wrong reasons. If working relentlessly is your thing, then you get to do it, no holds barred. No boss to please. No employees to harass. Just you doing what you love, burnout or not.

2. You get to keep what you make.

Yes, you have to pay taxes. Quite a bit, actually. On the other hand, your business profits are yours alone. You can choose to incorporate as an LLC or an S-corp, but either way, the money your business makes is the money that you make. Invest wisely.

3. You get to hire creatively.

Solopreneurs have help. They hire. They manage. They even get to boss people around, sort of. The process, however, is different. Instead of employing a CFO, the solopreneur might engage the services of an advisor, or purchase accounting SaaS [software as a service] or work with a contractor.

4. You discover the power of automation and outsourcing.

The entrepreneur *must* automate processes and outsource tasks. In the absence of minions to do his or her bidding, a successful solopreneur learns to create streamlined systems that accomplish crucial business tasks.

5. You live to work.

Solopreneurs don't *have* to go it alone. They can just as easily shutter their shops and start papering the town with their resumes. They can go right back to the corporate grind. But, why? Work is an adventure—a passionate engagement in the excitement of life. That's worth living for!

6. You can turn on a dime.

Startup companies love to *pivot.* Entrepreneurs pivot, too, and they can do so without any accountability to shareholders, stakeholders, board members, employees, investors or even a pet cat.

7. You choose everything about your business.

It takes a lot of decision-making to run the business. From the carpet's hue to the company's slogan, you decide *everything.* If you're a sucker for control, you've chosen the right line of work.

8. You can create your own schedule.

A 9-to-5, a 5-to-9, or a 9-to-9? What gives? You're the one in charge. Deciding how, when, where and how long to work is completely up to you. Most solopreneurs, though, don't choose to binge-watch Netflix, sleep in or loll, poolside. And "creating your own schedule" is just another way to describe the inflexibility and demands of working *all the time.*

9. You are responsible for your own success.

You have to take big risks if you want big rewards. Solopreneurs internalize this truth. Rather than leave their success to the whimsy of an employer, they choose to take their success firmly in hand.

10. You develop your own vision.

Whose vision do you want to follow? Your own or your employer's? A solopreneur makes this decision with fierce independence and experiences true fulfillment as a result.

11. Be your own brand.

Personal branding is the practice of creating and curating your public identity. Since a solopreneur *is* a business, he or she will find it more important than ever to engage and achieve personal branding.

12. You experience adventure every day.

An adventure is defined as "an unusual and exciting, typically hazardous, experience or activity." That basically sums up solopreneurship. Job security? Not a chance. Steady paycheck? Nope. Benefits? You're kidding. You live a life of adrenaline-pumping adventure, and you wouldn't have it any other way.

You need an extra hand when you run a small business. Someone to make a few sales calls. And order supplies that run low. Or do your weekly bookkeeping.

But what if you can't afford to hire, equip and create space for a full-time employee yet? Consider retaining a Virtual Assistant (VA) instead. With a VA, you can go back to focusing on your core pursuits. Leave the other stuff to these outsourced office professionals.

Source: www.entrepreneur.com/article/251738

The Lowdown on Virtual Assistants

A VA is an independent contractor who helps small businesses with their overflow. They work from their own offices (frequently home-based). They can help with many tasks that are usually handled by an in-house employee.

Sometimes entrepreneurs, and executives are hesitant because the investment (both monetary and of their time) is daunting, or they're not even sure what they'd be able to pass off to an assistant. But the most common excuse I sense—though most won't admit it—is that it's difficult to trust someone else with the business or work product.

The rise of the virtual assistant

According to *Forbes* magazine, virtual work has become increasingly popular among employees and employers. From 2005 to 2012, the number of telecommuting employees in the U.S. grew by 79.7 percent. And the number of self-employed workers is growing too—freelancers now account for over thirty-four percent of the total U.S. workforce.

Technology has allowed for workers to have more flexibility in their schedules and complete a wide range of tasks that don't require them to be physically present in an office. It also allows for businesses to access a huge talent pool that may not be readily available in their neighborhoods.

Release = Productivity

Knowing and understanding how to "scale" your business effectively is key to your productivity and your business' success. If it doesn't make sense to hire a full-time employee but having an extra hand on projects is essential to your growth, it's probably time to hire a virtual assistant.

There comes a time in an entrepreneur's life when he or she has to decide to 1) close the doors, 2) keep everything as is, or 3) scale to grow the business.

For many, scaling the business can be an exciting time, but also extremely stressful and overwhelming. What is scaling? How does one even go about scaling a business?

A company that has the opportunity of "scaling up" can manage its own growth when the time comes, because it has the *infrastructure* in place to do so. Very simply, scaling is making sure your foundation can handle the desired growth you're expecting. So when you are ready to scale your business, you are preparing for your *projected* desired growth and increase.

There are so many options out there, however the first step usually includes hiring employees and/or increasing your own workload, there's one solution that is increasing in popularity: hiring a virtual assistant (VA).

When you Should Hire a Virtual Assistant

A virtual assistant is a worthwhile investment for your startup or small business if you know how he or she can (and should) be utilized. If you fall into any of these categories, it might be time to consider a VA:

- You don't need and can't afford a full-time employee.

- You're having trouble completing your most important tasks.

- You need work done that doesn't require an office presence.

- You travel a lot and need someone who likes working virtually.

- You spend more time organizing rather than executing.

- You know what tasks need to be done but you don't have the manpower.

As with hiring any employee, finding a good fit is about addressing your individual business culture and goals. But if you know you need help with administrative tasks and you've got the flexibility to hire someone who can work remotely, it's definitely something worthwhile to consider.

Executives should...	A Virtual Assistant (VA) can...
Get out of the weeds	Pull tasks and projects off your to-do list
Spend more time monitoring projects	Remove scheduling and administration minutiae that preoccupies your time
Build new relationships to grow business	Find simple ways to expand your existing network

"The first step toward change is awareness.
The second step is acceptance."
- Nathaniel Branden

Asking for Help Is Tough

It's hard to let go of the reins and let someone else take over a piece of your business, especially if you've placed that trust in the wrong person before, and they've taken advantage of you. If you want to grow your business, you eventually have to stop doing it all yourself. You have to release some of that control, and you have to trust other people.

What can a VA do for YOUR business?

For many entrepreneurs, VAs offer an obvious benefit. They are a big timesaver during a phase in a company's growth where it may not be viable to have a full-time employee. Don't limit your scope to just personal assistant tasks—entrepreneurs use VAs for things like bookkeeping, data entry, social media, design, web development, email management, marketing administration and so much more.

Why Hire a VA?

If you need more help, that means your business is growing! Don't let it grow too wild and out of control before hiring a virtual assistant. Don't wait until you're struggling to get your head above water—at that point, it's already too late. Then when you add something else to your plate (like researching and hiring a VA), you will be likely setting that relationship up for failure.

Instead, look ahead at the bigger picture. If you're making a business plan for next quarter, think about the growth you hope to achieve and then ask yourself if you'll be able to manage all of that growth on your own. If the answer is no, which is likely, you'll want to add an assistant into that plan. Maybe you're doing fine now, but if you pick up ten more clients before the end of the year, you'll be working eighty to 100-hour weeks.

In the end, it comes down to one factor: INVESTMENT.

When it comes to hiring a VA, what you put in is what you're going to get out. If you invest your time into building a strong relationship with your virtual assistant, you're going to see all of these benefits and more.

Benefits of Hiring a Virtual Assistant

While there are many possible roadblocks, you might put in your own way, the benefits far outweigh the fear of actually hiring your virtual assistant. If you *don't* wait until you're panicking, if you *don't* cheat yourself out of a great opportunity by swearing you have the time to invest in building a relationship and then indulging self-sabotage by flaking, and if you *do* release some of the control and learn to trust your VA, then you'll definitely see your investment pay off.

There are some concrete benefits to hiring a virtual assistant.

1. No Salary Required

Okay. So the first time you receive a quote from a VA with their daily or membership rates, you start to sweat a little and a lump in the throat develops. We all second guess ourselves as soon as we have to shell out the dough, no matter what we're paying for (except for shoes! LOL).

But consider how much more that "retainer" would be if it were actually a salary that came with employee taxes and healthcare and Paid Time Off and… I mean, honestly, the extra expenses employees bring with them can be endless... not to mention the rent or lease expense from an actual brick-and-mortar location for them to work.

On top of that, say you've hired an employee to take care of administrative duties. That person may not have podcasting, social media, or copywriting in their skillset. What then? Do you hire someone else? Not if you are working with a virtual assistant company. They can actually build you a team for the same total price of work.

It's true! Hiring a VA may seem like a hefty investment before you really know how it will all shake out. But if you know you're committed to making it the best relationship it can be, you'll soon be looking for ways to make more money so that you can afford to add hours into your assistant's week.

2. Save Money

Budget is often top-of-mind for small business owners, which is why hiring a VA can be so attractive. Virtual assistants can be far less expensive in the long run than hiring employees because:

- The going rate is often less expensive than paying an employee's salary.

- You don't have to pay for office space and everything that comes along with it (such as tools and technology), as VAs are independent contractors who work remotely.

- You don't need to pay for benefits including insurance and over-time pay.

- Time is money. If you have a set list of tasks for your VA, document these processes to help save you time on training so that you can focus on other things.

- You only pay for what you need and don't waste time with underutilized employees.

Bottom line: If you can't afford someone full-time (or simply don't want to hire an employee), but your to-do list is growing at an unimaginable rate, then a VA could be the best choice for you.

3. Save Time

For small business owners, free time is seemingly non-existent. There is always something related to the business that requires attention, but the thing is, many of those tasks can easily be delegated to a VA. It can be hard to delegate at first, but by doing so you are able to:

- Reduce your workload.
- Stop worrying about the small tasks and start focusing on the business' core objectives.

The time saved can still be spent on your business (doing more of what you love), but it can be spent on more important things that actually require your attention—and that you actually like to do.

Make a list of what you have to do and a list of what you don't want to do or don't need to do. Anything that falls in that second column should be handed off to a VA. By outsourcing, you are able to release the burden of completing your endless list of tasks.

Letting go of some of your stress sounds like you might have hit the jackpot, right??

4. You're the Puppet Master

A VA can do more than simply schedule your meetings. She can be the third hand you always needed but never thought existed. She can (figuratively) jump inside your brain and predict your thoughts before you even think them. A mind reader of sorts.

If you take the time to let her into your daily workflow… if you share your preferences, show her your style of communication, explain to her why you do things a certain way, get all of the pet peeves that bug the crap out of you out of the way (so she takes note to never do them), and educate her about your company culture and values, you can indeed create a productive, efficient business "clone" of sorts.

A good VA will soak it all up like a sponge, write everything down in a Client Preferences document lest she ever forgets, and then begin to work within those boundaries that *you have* set.

5. You Have a Built-in Accountability Partner

When you're the business owner or executive in charge of an entire department, there's not likely going to be anyone (save maybe your spouse) who will challenge you when you're not doing what you said you were going to do. If you have a list of goals you'd like to complete each quarter, but you know you're not particularly good at keeping yourself accountable for those items, one of your assistants' jobs can be time management.

If you communicate with your VA exactly how you receive and react to accountability reminders, this person will be sure to phrase them or deliver them in a way that you will be receptive to. You won't hate your assistant, your goals will be met, and no one will fear for their jobs when they are trying not to say, "You told us you'd be revamping our content strategy LAST YEAR."

6. Take Your Workday Back

We're always asking or looking for more hours in the day. Here's your chance to get some of them back! If you could train someone to be the other half of your brain, would you? If you could impart all of your wisdom into this VA so that she knows how to answer your emails, book your meetings without asking you, or even proactively look for better solutions to the daily tasks you're already doing, doesn't that sound like a dream?

7. Expand Your Talent Pool

As an entrepreneur, odds are you have some pretty amazing skills up your sleeve. However, no matter how much you don't want to admit it, I'm pretty sure you're not that master of ALL skill sets for your business.

By hiring a virtual assistant you are able to expand the expertise in your business as many VAs often come with their own skill set, whether it be marketing, accounting, or something else entirely. Plus, it's not uncommon for VAs to work for other businesses while working for yours as well, and best practices they learn from other organizations can help your business in the long run.

In addition to expanding your company's knowledge base by hiring a VA who has expertise in an area you don't, you also have an unlimited talent pool to choose from. Being virtual, this person can be anywhere, meaning you aren't limited to the talent in your immediate area. Searching for a virtual worker means you can truly hire the best of the best to meet your needs.

FEAR (the elephant in the room)

Let's address it. As entrepreneurs, we are like first-time moms, protective of our developing babies. Finding the right assistant doesn't come around very often, and when they do, most entrepreneurs are constantly worried that they'll put in a ton of effort training and guiding assistants only to have their assistant leave for another opportunity. The amazing thing about working with a virtual assistant company is that if they happen to move on to another opportunity in life, the company will have the systems in place to train your new assistant *for you* with all of the knowledge you've already provided so that you don't have to do it again! It really is a win-win situation.

Services That VAs Provide

From data entry to event planning, live phone support, to schedule management, there are VAs available. Here are some of the services a VA can help with:

- Accounting/bookkeeping
- Advertising assistance
- Article drafting and submission
- Customer service support
- Database creation/management

- Desktop publishing, graphic design, presentation creation

- Internet and market research

- Meeting planning

- Public relations

- Social media updating and SEO

- Transcription and word processing

- Travel planning and booking

- Calendar management

- Scheduling

- Data Entry

- Concierge Services

- Event planning

- Conference team planning

Potato, Potatoe.

A temp, a VA, a contractor... Don't they do the same thing?

There is definitely some overlap between the terms temp or contractor and "Virtual Assistant." Temps tend to be temporary staff you retain through a placement agency or personnel firm. The temp normally works at your company's premises. He or she is paid by the staffing firm that represents them.

A contract worker is someone you hire directly. This person may be treated like an employee – you give them temporary space, equipment, even a job title – or you might have them work on a project remotely, using their own space and tools.

Virtual assistants are a form of independent contractors you almost never meet in person. More often than not, they perform administrative tasks and do so remotely.

Q-Tip #10 - Don't wait until you're struggling to keep your head above water to hire help. At that point, it's already too late.

Last but not least

I trust that you've enjoyed our time together, and that your brain is racing on ways to incorporate these best practices to start doing more of what you love. If you feel overwhelmed or like you have a lot to do alone, that is exactly the point. Use this book as your personal, pocket accountability partner.

When you are ready to engage a true accountability partner who can help you get organized, maximize your hours, focus on the most important parts of your business, follow-up with high-potential leads, and increase your bottom line, please reach out to my company Quintessential Executives. We specialize in helping business owners like you *do more of what you love.*

Visit us online at www.qexecs.com.

Thanks for reading!

Did you enjoy *The Quintessential Guide on How to Do More of What you Love for Entrepreneurs?*

Leave a review on Amazon and send us your review to: greener@qexecs.com.

Share this book title with the entrepreneurs you know.

Book Raquel Greene or Q Executives to help you organize your business or teach your team or existing administrative assistant.

About the Author

Raquel Greene is a career executive assistant with over fifteen years of experience in supporting and assisting C-level executives. She is also the founder of Quintessential Executives, which provides virtual support to business owners and CEOs. During her career, she has realized that, while wildly successful, very few executives embrace a lifestyle of work-life balance.. Her desire is to create a marriage between productivity and passion for the clients she supports. Visit QExecs.com to learn more.